Greetings Wally & Jeanne,
The events d[...]
However, when [...] the involvement of your friend please remember that authors tend to embellish certain circumstances. I believe it is called "library license."

your friend
Al

Steele's Amusements
Carnival Life on the Midway

by
Kenneth L. Miller

WALLY —
Buck said you've known each other for 71 years)!
More insight into his life —

Ken Miller

Copyright © 2013 by Kenneth L. Miller

All rights reserved. No part of this publication may be reproduced, distributed, or transmitted in any form or by any means, including photocopying, recording, or other electronic or mechanical methods, without the prior written permission of the publisher, except in the case of brief quotations embodied in critical reviews and certain other noncommercial uses permitted by copyright law. For permission requests, email the publisher, addressed "Attention: Permissions Coordinator,".

millerbooks, llc: kmiller@triton.net

Library of Congress Control Number: 2013915460

    Publisher's Cataloging-in-Publication Data

Miller, Kenneth L.
  Steele's amusements : carnival life on the midway / Kenneth L. Miller.
    p. cm.
  ISBN: 978-1-4921-0646-3 (pbk.)
  ISBN: 978-0-9898861-0-9 (e-book)
  Includes bibliographical references.
    1. Carnival owners—Middle West. 2. Carnivals—Middle West. 3. Indiana—Biography. I. Title.
GV1834.72.S74 2013
791.092—dc23
                                    2013915460

Disclaimer

This is a work inspired by the exploits of the Steele Family. It represents an oral history fraught with all the inaccuracies and inconsistencies typical of undocumented stories. Many conversations were as remembered or extrapolated from incomplete memories. Characters are combined and do not represent any one person living or dead.

*Dedicated to Maytha, Charlotte and Margaret Steele.
Three ladies that made the "...Show Beautiful"*

Introduction

On occasion, life makes an unexpected turn. These diversions usually end up being innocuous. They do no harm and also do no good. You adjust course and move on. After all, time is money. However, sometimes what seems at first a meaningless turn ends up opening a doorway to a *New World*. So was my introduction to the world of the carnival midway and my introduction to Steele's Amusements. I had known members of the Steele family for many years in a professional capacity but never probed into their history because that would have been prying. I am particularly good at prying, but never considered targeting a business associate or social friends with this dubious talent. Most people don't like uninvited guests peeking into their skeleton-laden closets. The Steele's are not like most people. The Steele family let me in, sat me down around the huge dining table and did what carnies do best. They told their stories. Just as carnival people do with each other when the crowds are gone and dinner is done, we sat near the fire bringing back everything that was deemed significant from a life on the road. What most people or carnival goers think of as significant about their experience is mainly not thought so by the carnies. You are on the outside of the looking glass, and from behind it, the carnival works on you. It's a show and it's a business. It truly is show business.

Four generations of Steeles dragged carnival rides, machinery, and unusual employees across the Midwest throughout the 1940's to the 1970's. They had created the archetypical traveling carnival with a combination of guts, fear, and entrepreneurial spirit. Their carnival started with a pony ride and developed into a corporation moving scores of trucks and employees to county fairs throughout the upper Midwest. The Steele family raised kids on the midway and produced lawyers, engineers, and most of all honest and interesting people. Fun people.

I first met Al (Buck) Steele when he came to a party my wife and I hosted at our home. I didn't know who the guy was, but that wasn't unusual, there were many people there I didn't know, so I just stood there doling out drinks. That is my job at these things. Later, I noticed that this guest was cracking up small groups of people by telling them carnival stories. I asked my wife if she knew who he was. She explained that Al Steele, the carny had come to our door and said that he had checked us out with 'Tico' and decided we were 'O.K.' people, that we were hard workers. I started to absorb the novelty of having a carnival-type person run *me* through a vetting process before coming to my home. Most people would have worked that the other way. This particular Steele, unknown to me previously, had come bearing gifts: a load of stories gathered over decades of carnival work. I asked my wife, "Who was this 'Tico' that vouched for us?" She said, "I guess Tico is your lawyer. He's Al Steele's cousin. He grew up in the carnival."

"You mean R. Lawrence Steele, Esq. former United States Attorney for the Northern District of Indiana? The guy appointed by President Reagan to a high Justice Department position? Tico?" Tico had given us his stamp of approval. Carnies had infiltrated the highest levels of government.

In successive years we met many times with Buck Steele, and heard more of the carnival life. We laughed until adult beverage ran from our noses and tears ran down our cheeks. After these sessions my jaw would ache from laughing. As in all storytelling, delivery is everything. Certainly the Steele's as a group can lay out a story with the right context and make you laugh. My wife suggested I write these stories down and try to recreate some of the fun that the now closed carnival still generated.

Steele's Amusements is meant to walk a reader through the midway and see things from a carny perspective and relive some of the more interesting events of life on the midway.

The carnival business is seen through the lens of mid and late 20th century popular culture. Changing attitudes in society about disability were profoundly felt at Steele's and from the '60's the operation downplayed sideshow freaks and oddities, but these facets of carnival life could not be eliminated entirely. People had certain expectations of what a carnival was and what they expected to see. Steele's kept pace with the times by reworking themes and adding attractions to suit changing tastes, while always keeping one foot in the past. This was a business necessity and also *homage* to their eldest, L.E. Steele. Grandpa Steele, as L.E. was known to most, was a Great Depression entrepreneur, taking his humble photography business and making the adjustments necessary to survive in the cold, industrial Midwest.

I have learned a number of things in my research of carnivals in general and *Steele's Amusements* specifically: Don't waste your sympathy on carnival people. They are a proud lot that knows only too well about the life they lead. More than most, they are an accepting group. Carnies hope to make money by entertaining. They don't care a whole lot just how that is done. This is not highbrow entertainment and carnival people don't have the posture to stick their noses in the air. To them the carnival sideshow was simply a part of the economic engine. For this reason, carnival people never looked down on the disabled, but rather admired them for what they brought to the show.

Carnival freaks of years ago were fairly proud of their independence from charity. They disdained those that hounded them out of show business with over-wrought guilt. The 'do-gooders' of the normal world did more *harm* than good by shaming the carnival family out of the sideshow business. The 'freaks' found the carnival sideshow a safe haven where they could make a living in an accepting atmosphere. The carnies took people from the downside of privilege and gave them a chance too often refused by the rest of the working world.

Sometimes the carnival provided a place to hide or a time to rest. The old concept of running away from your troubles by joining a traveling carnival was very often true. Carnival people don't dwell on your past if you don't judge them on theirs. I haven't met a carny yet that regretted being one.

The more exposed you are to a carnival operation, the more obvious it becomes that *this is terrifically hard work*. Carnival workers have to setup the games, rides, tents and booths no matter what the weather. At all costs, the business must open on time, and the show must go on. Just because it's pouring rain and you're standing in a foot of mud today, doesn't mean that you can put off the show until tomorrow. The work is hot, heavy and backbreaking, but somehow, some people can pull it off year after year. These people have guts, and through it all, they have heart.

My hope is to tell these stories of carnival life with some of their inherent humor. Nothing can take the place of hearing them directly from the horse's mouth, but the carny is loathe to put things on paper. This will have to do.

A Brief History of the Steele Industry:

L.E. Steele was in a tight spot. The Depression had landed with a thump in Northwest Indiana and his portrait photography business wasn't pulling in enough dough to feed the bulldog. L.E., the progenitor of Steele's Amusements, the carnival *"Show Beautiful,"* had an eye for expansion born from the necessity to eat. The scrappy Steele had a small photography studio in Hammond, Indiana smack in the middle of the rust belt, but needed more lucrative work to support his family. He needed to find enough work to last him all year long. You couldn't do this working in one place, not during the Depression, so L.E. went on the road. L.E. would snap portrait photos all over the Great Lakes states in places like Cedar Lake, Indiana, where Al Capone and other notable Midwesterners liked to hang out in the 1930's. This was a resort area that needed vacation pictures. Girls in overly modest swimming suits would prance around this small resort lake community and L.E. Steele would take tasteful pictures that they could send home to their sweethearts or make into postcards. It was a natural jump for Steele to set up his photography booth at local carnivals. He was able to find a ready supply of customers who wanted to memorialize their visit to the fair and would pay for a portrait. L.E. kept his eyes open and wanted to expand his income with other carnival activities. The carnival, Steele surmised, was depression proof, even recession proof, like bars and speakeasies of the time. The carnival midway drew in people for cheap entertainment *paid for in cash.*

Steele decided to travel with a *40-miler*, a carnival that operated within forty miles or so if its home base or what carnies call Winter Quarters. These small carnivals were common in the 1930's and 1940's when the traveling carnival was at its zenith.

L.E. went out with Bodart's Shows and was real proud of it. He had found an occupation that he was good at.

Bodart's was out of Shawano, Wisconsin, the claimed hometown of Senator Joseph McCarthy. Why Shawano would claim Joe McCarthy when his real hometown of Grand Chute seldom did is a mystery, but this is very conservative country. This is also dairy country, where the only thing hated more than communism was oleo.

L.E. procured a group of eight ponies and built a pony ride. Ponies were a good bet as a starter ride because parents might also go for a professional photo of the little tyke screaming through his first equine experience. There was no evidence that L.E. went too deeply into the pony pose route but the potential was there. Steele was always aware of potential and always willing to ring up a sale. He also started exhibiting a very consistent Steele trait: a mechanical inclination expressed in the *constant* tinkering with what you have to make something you don't. He figured out a way to tether the ponies independently so that when one was employed, the off-duty ponies could rest. This helped save on wear and tear of the animals and saved on pony shoes. Along with the Pony Ride, L.E. set up a Shooting Range. The old kind with heavy metal moving targets, ducks, chicks, bears and the like would crank past the view of a player. Young sharpshooters would blast . 22 caliber bullets at L.E.'s targets raising a din.

The Pony Ride was successful and L.E., never a particularly happy man, at least knew he could support his family at 25¢ a ride. He brought his kids into the business and their kids too, eventually.

Al Jr., L.E.'s grandson grew up under the Bodart carnival sign and knew what it was like to be a small cog in the bigger establishment. Al was given the carny name, "Buck" and was known by that name most of his life. Buck remembered his earliest carny slight: "When Bodart, a real short guy but plenty tough was bitching about the level of dissension in the show. He had everybody come down for the bally (speech, you know, *ballyhoo*) on the sideshow. It was kind of a wet day and he had all of the ride boys and all the people in the carnival, probably about eighty people, stand in front of him as he gave them Hell. They weren't doing anything right and acting wild and crazy. So Bodart, acting as little Hitler let 'em have it. "Hell, there's something wrong with every one of you or you wouldn't be here." Buck was embarrassed for his mom who was standing there taking the abuse surrounded by the rest of the family. Buck heard the message: "There was something wrong with each one of us. How far can a carny expect to go in this life?"

By the early 1940's, L.E. Steele had put together a substantial group of carnival games and small rides. His son, Al Sr. added a Milk Bottle joint, Balloon Dart joint, Cork Shooting Gallery, and a penny arcade. He, his son and grandson jumped or *hopscotched* in carny lingo, to various fairs and carnivals in rapid succession. To Tip-Top Shows, Snapp's Shows, and worked on and off with Ernie Farrow who started Farrow's Shows. Throughout the year, L.E.'s family would work in Valparaiso, Indiana at a bearing factory.

When the Japs hammered Hawaii in 1941, the Steele boys were ready to do their duty, but only Uncle Ray ended up going to the South Pacific. The other brothers, Al Sr. and Vinnie were automatically deferred from the service without any say in the matter. They worked for an important defense supplier and had to stay put.

After the war, L.E. got sick and needed some help to handle his obligations at Bodart's carnival. His son, Al Sr. jumped into the breach to cover him. The elder Al took his kid, Al Jr., a.k.a. Buck to fill in for gramps. A lesson in carnival economics began here. Al Sr. was just going to run the Cork Shooting Gallery and the Penny Arcade for L.E.. The deal was for twenty percent of the take from the games in cash. The factory workers' eyes opened up when, after just six weeks he had more money in his pocket than if he had worked at the factory all year. Al Sr. never finished high school, but was smart enough to figure this much out: If running one joint was this profitable, how about…six?

Ray, back from the meat grinder war in the Pacific was

ready to jump into the carnival fray as well. He pulled together a couple of kiddie or *punk* rides, a Tank Rider and a Sky Fighter, and built a hot dog grab joint. As time went on, the Steeles comprised more of someone else's carnival than that carnival could stand. It was a basic conflict of interest to hire in a large group of games and rides that would compete with the carnival's own. Something had to give.

Al Steele, Sr. decided to take the plunge and form his own carnival, *Steele's Amusements*. In 1958, after hocking his soul to buy the rest of the rides and equipment he needed, he prepared to go on the road. He negotiated the purchase of rides from Snapp's carnival of Joplin, Missouri. Two hard heads came together but a deal was finally struck and Steele's was ready to make a go of it. Snapp told Al Sr. that after he paid for the rides, *in cash only*, the show dates would be arranged and Steele's would be all set to start on the road. The problem was that Snapp didn't end the negotiation a happy man. He sold the equipment to Steele at the end of the season without booking the show dates as he had promised. Steele's had a show but no place to put it on. This was a bad cash flow situation for an upstart business, but the hounds were at Al Sr.'s back and the incentive was in place to succeed or starve. Snapp twisted the knife as he said goodbye to Al Steele,

Sr.: "I didn't book the spots for you. I've got your money. Screw you." Snapp, who had *the* major show in Wisconsin, had virtually assured Steele's failure.

There sat the Steele clan, with "a whole backyard full of trucks, nothing hardly to eat on, and no place to work for the summer." Al Sr. packed up the kids and headed for northern Wisconsin. At least he knew how to survive there at his cabin on the Wisconsin River. Al Sr. did odd jobs and whatever came along while his brothers, Vinnie and Ray went on the convention circuit lining up spots. The thought of failure, and the bank, and creditors made it mandatory they hit the ground running in this new business venture. It was a race to see what happened first, Steele's making some money or the bank coming for the rides.

Spring came and Steele's Amusements went on the road. What was meant to be a *forty-miler* became more like a *250-miler*. Steele's had to range far from Winter Quarters to survive, but decided that to stand still was to fail. In 1966, Steele's negotiated with Ernie Farrow of Farrow's Shows to buy their rides. Ernie was sick. He was losing blood from somewhere and couldn't muster the energy he needed to run his carnival. To help him, Steele's acquired the rides, equipment and Ernie himself for a while. Even partially depleted of blood, Ernie Farrow was still the toughest guy on the block. A Golden Gloves boxer, at 5'-4" he was gonna put your lights out if you gave him trouble. In the carnival business, this kind of enforcement attitude is generally considered a good thing. Disputes have to be handled quickly so the show can go on without interruption. Ernie was 120 lbs. of law and order on the midway. Coupled with Ray Steele, another tough guy, discipline was maintained at the end of a right hook.

Steele's put Ernie Farrow's name on the sign and toured as a combined outfit. They developed a group of summer regulars to run the games and rides. Business people, teachers, relatives, friends and college kids would join up for a season to run joints and travel the Midwest. After Al Sr. passed away, his son Buck took over and encouraged friends to send their kids to work a summer in the carnival. Nothing promoted independent thinking more than a young person living on the road for a few months. Sure, sometimes a *prissy* sort of kid would come on the carnival; like the time that one boy came with his entire suburban uniform. From the penny loafers to the button down collar shirt, the boy was seemingly from a different planet. This was not a preppy summer job, and this guy had made a wrong turn somewhere. He even brought a bathrobe. Aside from the ridicule he received for such civilized ways, in all other respects he was treated O.K. After all, he was under the protective carnival tent. Rule number one in the carny mental notebook: Take care of your own and *your own* means anyone working with the carnival. It may seem like a Mafia cabal to the local cops, but it's a family to the people with the tents. Even if you have to beat the tar out of a ride boy to keep him straight, he's protected from outsiders. *Carnival property.* Once Buck's mom, Maytha and Aunt Charlotte were asked to come to a cocktail party and be checked out by potential summer help donors. The people were university professors considering letting their kid travel with Steele's Amusements for a season. The two carny ladies went to the party expecting the third degree and not a little apprehensive that they were trespassing into another class structure. What the university professor/parents saw were two more caring parents willing to protect their kid for a summer. Maytha and Charlotte passed inspection. The kid they took in for the summer grew up to be the CEO of a $100 Million insurance company in Merrill, Wisconsin. No worse for wear by working the midway.

The favor Buck did for Ernie Farrow in 1966 was returned in 1976. Buck's wife was diagnosed with cancer and he had to be with her. He had to come off the road. Buck asked Ernie to take his boys on tour and run things while he dealt with the worst time in his life. Farrow took on the carnival and later bought his rides and equipment back. Buck Steele ended his run with the carnival by coming full circle. Farrow's Shows still runs today throughout the country with some of Steele's Amusements still inside, spinning kids and pushing popcorn.

Hillsboro, Wisconsin

"We've got Baby Flo Johnson! Alive! Alive! Alive! She's so big, she's so round it takes ten men to hug 'er and a boxcar to lug 'er! She's 816 pounds of screamin' big fat Detroit Soul Mama! Come in and see her ALIVE!"

Buck Steele was sitting on the hood of the Ford and assessing progress. The calendar said it was the 1960's, but the routine was unchanged from a decade before. Cousin Tommy had already started belting out his practice sideshow barker routine, but Buck was looking for more tangible signs that *Steele's Amusements* was ready to put on *"The Show Beautiful."* That was what it was called then. It was on the banner and painted on the carnival trucks. Harry Crippins, between bottles of really cheap whiskey had done a passable job of putting the Steele's logo on everything he could find. Buck's granddad had deftly stolen the slogan from Bodart's carnival back in the '40's as a symbol of defiance or maybe a symbol of *screw you* to his former employer. Old L.E. Steele learned a thing or two from his stint with Bodart's and the catchy subtitle was one of them.

Their caravan of twenty-four semi-tractors and house trailers had rolled into Hillsboro, Wisconsin early, real early and Uncle Ray had done his usual job of preparing the fairgrounds and laying out the carnival midway. The location of each trailer, ride, sideshow tent and carny game had to be staked out. This thing fitted together like a three acre Chinese puzzle and Uncle Ray was the guy making it fit. When done, you couldn't stick a hair between the trailers, they were so carefully set. That was a good thing, because trouble always tried to seep through those cracks between trailers and trouble is not what Steele's wanted.

Buck slid off the hood and started to slog through the mud. It was deep and getting deeper, fed from the constant rain that had begun over a day ago. They were all tired. This was one of the last stops of the summer tour and it just *would* have to be this wet. Labor Day weekend in Southern Wisconsin. Save the hardest for last. Today was the *Hell day* of carnival life. Setup day. It was hot, humid and the fairgrounds were as muddy as Hell. Buck and the crew could deal with the mud, but it still wasn't a pleasant Wisconsin experience behind the Cheddar Curtain.

"Enjoying yourself, Buddy?" Buck stuck to his cheery, sarcastic greeting.

"*Sure* Buck." Buddy referred to Al by his official carny name. It was typical carny behavior to overly exaggerate politeness in the face of adversity. "Say, Buck, who gets the credit for booking this shit hole?"

"The credit and pleasure is all mine, Bud. Do you need anything else?"

"Yeah, you owe me a hammer, I dropped mine and it sunk in a foot of muck." Buddy was still grinning.

"Maybe you ought to see a doctor or something if you keep losing your grip on things. Hope it doesn't affect your sex life, Buddy." Buck moved on. Buddy ran the *Shoot the Star* and it wouldn't do to rile him up too much. They use real bullets at that shooting range game. Buck remembered working with his granddad, L.E., years back. L.E. Steele started with a pony ride and a shooting gallery in 1947. Since then one Steele or another had been beating tracks between northern Wisconsin and northern Indiana, setting up, working in, and tearing down carnival shows. At first it was a slow, insidious crawl into the carnival business.

Granddad eased into it with the pony ride and then bought one of the big old metal shooting galleries, the kind that had rows and rows of metal ducks and bears that made a big racket when you shot them down. After a while, L.E. went chicken and got rid of the bullets in favor of a cork gallery. Buck always figured his granddad just got tired of standing in front of some crazed Badger State marksman loaded up with .22 shells and Old Style beer. No matter the real reason, the cork gallery won out and grandson Buck was tapped to run the game. That was the beginning. Now Albert Steele, Jr. (Buck) ran the whole shebang and most of his family was involved too. The carnival had grown much bigger, adding rides and attractions every year. But it had lost some of the old standards of the carnival midway. No hootchy-kootchy! L.E. had the basic componentry for a swell peep show, from some moderately risqué photos of ripe Wisconsin girls plucked from his photography business to a penny arcade to show them in. Then there was the standard hot tent spiel…"Red hot saucy girls! Not your girl next door! No sir! You want to see the girl next door you would'a stayed at home! Boys, these girls are gonna put on a dance for you that you'll never forget. No, this isn't a church dance and you won't see any white gloves here. These girls, and notice I'm not calling them ladies, are gonna show you some things you can't tell mom about. Red hot and getting' hotter, next show in five minutes!" Buck thought it was just another aspect of traditional carny business killed off by a changing society. In fact, most of the sideshow biz was falling out of favor. Why pay to see oddities or freaks when you can see them walking down the street for free? Tattoo man? Nothing new there. Tall, short, fat, skinny, stupid? We have the NBA for three of those and Weight Watchers for the other two. Things are a changin'. The term 'freaks' now referred to those of the 'Woodstock Generation' that ingested something called *windowpane*.

Buck was considering the need to get a CAT bulldozer in to move the trucks around. They were sinking into the mud just as soon as a driver let up on the gas pedal. Time was running short for setup and it wouldn't be the first time he needed to haul in heavy equipment to keep from becoming part of Wisconsin fossil history. Once, a few years back he had to rent a 'dozer to drag all of the rides and trucks out of the mud on tear down day. Buck's mom, Maytha still talks about the lousy vacuum operated windshield wipers slopping mud back and forth on the old Ford. Buck had to lie to the equipment rental guy: "*Sure*, I know how to operate the bulldozer! It's been a little while though. See, usually I, um, am more used to running a Deere than a CAT..." The rental agent was pretty skeptical. Here this carnival guy that he had never seen before, wanted his most expensive piece of equipment. "Well, I'm gonna have to see you run the machine, you know, check you out and also this is gonna take a sizable deposit."

"Nah! I only need the thing for an hour or so and we don't have the cash drawers open. Tell you what, come see me unload the 'dozer from it's trailer if you want and I can show that I can be trusted with it. I have to get moving now or all the equipment in the world won't help. Hey, you ever get over to Janesville? Let me give you a few books of complimentary tickets..." Buck was smoothing over the rough spots in the negotiation, greasing another wheel.

"O.K., but I have to have the thing back by closing today, otherwise we gotta get a deposit." The rental guy succumbed even though he didn't want to lend his 'dozer out to just any numbskull. The fake worked.

The rental guy was a Czech or Bohemian as some of them like to be called. Generally these European transplant types are pretty easy to get along with, if not a little on the suspicious side. Apparently Hitler's legacy was to make the Czech people a little wary of anyone wanting to 'borrow' something from them. On the other hand, they *have* provided Wisconsin with the best beer-making technology and the ability to consume it.

Buck climbed into the cab of the monster machine and learned damn quick how to move the thing and look professional about it. It was either learn the machine in five minutes or be stuck in the stinking muck with all the crew and the kids for days. Twelve hours later he was an expert with the CAT.

"Jesus, this place smells like a barnyard and that's the good news." Buck noticed that the more rain that fell the more hay the grounds people were throwing down. Mixing that with the usual amount of fair droppings and some heat would make this week memorable. It was time to set up the Ferris Wheel.

This was painful. Tommy was practicing at the microphone again. Cousin Tommy Steele was aspiring to be a professional carnival sideshow talker. In the biz, nobody called them 'barkers' anymore. They're 'talkers' and Tommy was working at it. Tommy's voice wasn't of the correct pitch to carry over the Steele's Amusements P.A. system. He *had* worked out the beat. The rhythm of the bark was the most important thing. It had to stop passers by. It had to garner interest in something they may have no interest in at all. It had to grab them and make them stand in murderous Midwestern July heat to see something unusual. What could be more unusual than a woman that weighed as much as a Volkswagen? Well, plenty, but Tommy was going to work Baby Flo for all she was worth. This was his break in the business. *Show business*.

The weather was holding a little so maybe the Ferris Wheel would go up O.K. Buck snapped out of his trance and felt for a cotter pin in his hat. Carny guys always keep extra cotter pins in their hats, jeans, or whatever. A missing cotter pin can amount to a small fry plunging from great heights to the feet of his/her terrified parents. This could almost assure a cancellation of the contract for the next year and also cause a nasty safety audit by the Wisconsin Industrial Board folks. You never knew when an inspector would notice a pin missing on a ride. This Ferris Wheel was always tricky to set up. The wind had to be on your side to erect the big wheel and your help had to be halfway sober. Maybe Tommy would knock off the prattle so they could concentrate. Any distraction while you were standing on a one-inch piece of steel forty feet in the air was a problem. Slick was weaving around and looked bad. He was just putting the last of his 24 bottles of beer, the empty bottle back in the case. Buck needed him to hold the rope while he put up the Big Wheel. If he yanked the rope too hard it would knock him right out of the structure and Buck was getting nervous. "I gotta really be careful today", Buck yelled to

Slick. "I can handle it, Buck." He was enough of an alcoholic he *could* handle it too. So up went the Ferris Wheel.

Buck climbed and planted his feet on a cross-member. The Ferris Wheel began to move. Hope there was no lightning in the weather forecast. On the ride, Buck felt one of his cotter pins drop below and disappear into the top layer of mud.

Tommy was hitting his stride. He was barking for hot dog sales, coke sales, popcorn; you name it. There was a rhyme to it. "If you're in line you're on time! But if you wait, you're gonna be late!" Tommy had the pedigree all right. He was a third generation carnival family member wanting to work with the big boys. He just had to get that pituitary to kick in, or anything to kick in. Sensing that Tommy's testosterone couldn't be relied upon immediately, Buck's dad, Al Sr. came up with some suggestions. First, he said Tommy would have to use a falsetto voice that would project out over the P.A. system and the midway. Al Steele Sr. was a showman and knew the value of bringing in customers by piquing their interest. God help you if you lost enthusiasm, drive, or the will to sell the product. Baby Flo was the product and this was, after all, a business. Tommy assumed a tenor pitch and ran the bark over and over. It would work. Baby Flo would continue to be barked or talked by her husband, a man of normal dimensions, but Tommy had studied the bark: A sideshow barker in waiting.

Buck was 35 feet up in the Ferris Wheel standing on a wet, slick support. He could hear Tommy still warming up the vocal cords. There was some comfort in hearing the same routine over time. It links the past, when Al Sr. was alive to now. Buck's dad died at the age of forty-eight of lung cancer, never smoked a day in his life. Figure that.

"We got a loaf of bread and a pound of meat! All the mustard you can eat! They're rarin' red-hot with the pickles in the middle and the mustard on top! By golly they're good! Get a lunch of a foot-long hot dog and an ice cold drink!" Tommy again.

Uncle Ray was always experimenting with hot dogs, bratwurst and cooking things in beer. Ray was in charge of the whole organizational effort of setup. After that when the carnival was ready to work, Ray and his wife Charlotte ran the grab joints like the hot dog-popcorn-corn dog business. Ray was known far and wide as a tough man. He was a World War II veteran and a survivor of battle on Okinawa. Now he was the top dog in the world of the hot dog. He developed the hot dog bark and carefully engineered the food sales strategy. Simply stated, the Marine *made* people buy hot dogs. Ray would say, "You guys have GOT to start creating a crowd." The carnie's main marketing strategy is concerned with making the *'tip'* or crowd. If the crowd is there, sales will follow. If you didn't know how to create this tip, Ray would step in and make it happen. Nobody likes to stand in line, but anybody that could survive the Marine battle on Okinawa could certainly make a few people wait for a corn dog. Ray's son, Larry worked the hot dog wagon and developed a show to work the tip. He was a flat-assed great dancer and would do the classic James Brown dance moves like the 'turnaround' and the 'breakdown', with hands full of hot dogs and corn dogs. Larry leveraged that skill as an attorney and later as U.S. Attorney; a skilled performer. Larry and Cousin Tommy held down the hot dog stand together and learned to sell. People would be watching, entertained and forget they were standing in line. They worked the tip at the hot dog stand just like working it at the Dart Game. Keep 'em buying hot dogs... They would take corn dogs, dip them in batter, flip more batter in the air and catch it on the way down. There is an art to corn dog work. It is performance art.

With the two big generator trucks in place, heavy electrical line was being strung to light the place up. Smitty the electrician was helping Uncle Ray haul the cable to junction boxes in back of the rides. This left everyone with a queasy feeling because the rain was still falling at intervals and the electrical connections were spending at least some of the time under muddy water. "What OSHA doesn't know won't hurt 'em" was the reply if anybody was stupid enough to ask about it. The electrical hookups were always a little tricky, but the real men worried more about lightning frying a Ferris Wheel load of kids or a power line coming into contact with a ride going up on setup day. Ray's brother Vinnie had engineered a crane truck to erect rides a few years ago. Last year, while four guys were up in the Tilt-A-Whirl the thing smacked right into a zillion-volt line running above the fairgrounds. Al thought that they were looking at four dead men, but for some reason they all fell out of the machine like monkeys from a tree. They were a bit dazed, but otherwise unimpaired. Worker's comp. claim averted. Most of the people involved with Steele's lived under some similar, lucky star. Most, but not all.

  The rides were moving into place according to Uncle Ray's plan. It all looked like an elongated figure '8' with the generators in the middle to feed each end of the midway. The front end of the show, nearest to the entrance held all of the game booths called 'joints'. The general idea was to put the big show stoppers like the giant Ferris Wheel way in the back so that marks or customers would spend their money on their way to the final destination, the big rides. Ticket booths up front and in the back kept the money flowing. These were often places where trusted family members worked. Buck's daughter learned to handle a ticket booth from the age of eight. From end-to-end Steele's Amusements was a family affair. L.E. Steele started it, worked it and died. Buck's dad, Al Sr. the same. Buck's wife was in it and his daughter was in it. His Uncles Ray, and Vinnie were in it and his cousins Larry, Randy, Tommy, and Judy. His mom, Maytha was in it big time and so were Buck's Aunts Charlotte and Margaret. In all, some seventeen Steele's were involved in the carnival. One aspect of such deep family involvement is that if you screw something up the whole family is affected and disappointed in you. So you just can't screw up. After Buck's dad died, he was thrust into running the family business. It was where he wanted to be. His dad had wanted him to finish law school and do something else. Buck did finish law school but didn't want to do anything else. This was where the action was. Never a dull carny moment.

The Ferris Wheel went up without mishap. The weather didn't get any worse. It was time to round up the ride guys. The carnival had about three hours left to go until showtime.

Cousin Tommy was working the Six-Cat Game tonight and maybe pushing it a little. He was barking out a particularly challenging sales pitch when a well-lubricated Wisconsin man stepped up to the counter. The Six-Cat is one of those old-time, 'you knock the fuzzy little kitties down and win' games. It's not rigged, exactly, just made more difficult by making the target look larger than it is. When you through the ball at the cats it will just brush by the fuzz trim of the cat and leave the thing standing in place. The only way to win it is to hit the stuffed cat dead center and hard. The player was drunk, but not enough to affect his aim on the first two throws. Buck, observing the game from a few feet away saw that the player was really getting full of himself and had a good chance of winning. Tommy on the other hand had absolutely no intention of letting this Cheddar Head win the game and was really turning up the distractions. "Hey, Pal, you want to make it best out of six for the big prize? You wanna make any side bets? Hey who is that guy with your girlfriend?" Tommy was shouting in the guy's ear with no effect. He kept trying to distract him, acting like an overly excited hophead. Tommy was jerking, weaving and waving his arms. "Hey, what are you spastic?" The player spat out. "Get outta my face! I'm gonna win this thing." Tommy's agitated act still was not working. He couldn't throw the player off rhythm. The only thing left was to physically obstruct his throw. Buck saw this coming. Tommy was just young enough to try something stupid to keep from losing a 'piece of plush' as the stuffed animals are called. Buck flinched as he saw Tommy whack the player on the head with a small pink and white Teddy Bear as the guy wound up for his final throw. That did it. This, now purple-faced player, dove for Tommy. Tommy vaulted the adjacent side counter of the game booth and commenced an all out sprint to the other end of the midway. The player, scooping up a pile of balls as he pursued, started lobbing them with all his might at Tommy. The player's third throw did hit its target, bouncing off of Tommy's head. Tommy was picking up steam as Buck and several other carnies tried to close on the infuriated player. "You gotta hand it to the guy, he really can throw…" Buck thought as he moved forward. Somebody was gonna have to knock this guy down before he killed Tommy. The kid was ducking and bobbing all the way down two hundred yards of midway. Thing is, he was gonna run out of room some time. Tommy sped past Little Dora Willard the Cyclops Girl and felt another fastball smack him in the neck. This was starting to hurt. The end of the midway was closed off by fencing that went around the back of the Tilt-a-Whirl. The pursuit was about to end with Tommy's escape blocked. The young carny was about to get his clock cleaned. As this unfolded, Buck was coming up from behind and the carny running the Tilt-a-

Whirl figured things out fast. He threw the brakes on the spinning ride and jumped into the fray from the control platform. Ditto for two other ride guys and in a moment, *Steele's Raiders* was formed. A phalanx of burley carnies took stance between Tommy and the screaming Six-Cat player. The biggest ride guy wrapped a tattooed arm around the player's neck and pressed a sleeper hold into effect. Player crumbles like stale potato chips. Sure, Tommy was wrong in jerking the player around, but this was family. Certainly, as a matter of Wisconsin common law, you can't kill a kid for smacking you with a Teddy Bear. Buck leaned over the subdued player and calmly spoke to him. "Hey, Pal, why don't you cool down. The race is over. If you want, you can have any prize on the board. This is the carnival for Christsakes. We're supposed to be having fun here."

"The sons-a-bitch hit me with the Teddy Bear." The player said. There was just no way of saying this without sounding stupid and the gathered carnies cracked up. Laughing until snot ran out of their noses, the carnies boosted the player to his feet and dispersed. Sometimes laughing can defuse a situation, sometimes not. Buck figured it went about fifty-fifty.

As the irate Cheddar-Head left to get a corn dog, Buck lit into Tommy for leaving his station. "If you're so damned worried about losing one piece of plush, what about leaving the 'Six' and people walking off with *all* your merchandise? Smart-assed kid. Actually, you better get back, all this attention is usually good for business. People wanna see if you got your ass kicked. Put on a show for 'em and maybe mess up your clothes a bit. You know, add some *drama*."

As Buck moved on to check the ticket booths, Tommy walked back to the 'Six-Cat' to resume business. Dozens of players were waiting to try their hand at knocking down the fuzzy little cats.

Rockford, Illinois

Uncle Ray was running ahead of the rest with his crew. Ray was the lot manager. His mission was to establish a beachhead on the fairgrounds and mark out trailer locations, joint slots and concession areas. The midway was under complete control of Ray Steele. Screw with Ray Steele and you might just end up with the worst spot on the grounds, the donniker; the toilet of business locations. It was his to give and give he would.

Two days into the fair, a still spot on Kishwaukee Avenue, rumors started to circulate about a gang fight coming. Two competing groups of hillbillies, the cops said, might try to iron out their differences in a vacant lot near the midway. It was approaching dark, and the joints were in full swing; hot dogs, cotton candy and the whole nine yards.

Two cars pulled into the vacant lot next to the midway. Each was loaded with white trash carrying baseball bats and small firearms. This largely went unnoticed by the carnival workers as they attended their jobs. Moments later a bullet ricocheted from a large oak tree right on the midway. The concessionaires were all yelling at uncle Ray asking what was happening and what to do. Other carnies were getting the kids under cover and searching for weapons to defend themselves. Several more shots rang out and more tree bark and dirt went flying. The shooting gallery guy pulled the chain locking up the guns. He handed out .22 rifles to other concessionaires and ride guys. Other concession workers pulled out their own personal guns and took cover where they could. Ray's service .45 automatic appeared in his hand. He must have had it in his trailer near by. Ray racked the slide back on his .45 and shrank to a stooping position. This wasn't Okinawa, but it felt like it for the moment. With his ass six inches from the ground, his gun arm pointed straight up, his legs started to roll fast. This is what it took to be one of the 17 survivors of his company on blood soaked Japanese soil. Would it work in Rockford? Ray didn't even think about it. He never did. The one consistent adjective used for Uncle Ray was that he was fearless. If you think about anything too much, fear can creep into the equation, but not for Ray. His legs pumped faster than anyone had seen before. He burned ground over to the phone booth. *Trouble.* What carny doesn't have change on him for the phone? Ray. A few more bullets were banging off of trees along the midway, and Ray retraced to the nearest change apron. Coined up, he cruised back to the phone booth. The cops went code three as soon as Ray dropped the phone. The punks with the baseball bats and hardware made a run for it as soon as the sirens could be heard. Two cars burned dirt and left. Crisis resolved by the Marine, once again. Fearless.

   Moms working the midway put away their butcher knives and the small kids came out from under tables in the trailers. A ride guy put his weaponized steel lever back on the Rock-O-Plane. Concessionaires put back their pistols, tire irons, and huge crescent wrenches. Another day at the fair was drawing to a close.

Ride Guys and Jointees

"35 bucks a day and cigarettes!" The screening mechanism to select ride operators was not as tough as it could have been. It tended to draw people from a certain slice of American society. This is a male only job category. The "help wanted" ad read something like..."Have you just a) gotten out of prison b) gotten out of the armed forces or c) graduated junior high school...if you're 18 years old and have a drivers license or plan to get one, come see us out on U.S. Route 30!" These were not violent people, although one ride guy had stated that his life's ambition was to kill someone. He was in the minority. He kept his job with the carnival because you never knew when you might need somebody like that, Buck decided. There was the ride guy that killed his friend in

Florida over a juke box selection, but he was with a different carnival. Sure, there was the guy that used to beat his wife and then she shot him three times. Buck remembered that one well. Hank was shot in the wintertime. Actually he was shot in the chest and abdomen but it was during the winter. He was a real thick chested, barrel chested guy on the outside, but seemed nice enough. A real cupcake that looked like a mob guy. He was married to Sally and she was as meek as they come. Some called Sally small and mousy. Hank would beat the Hell out of her when the mood struck him. One day when he had gotten done beating her, she picked up a gun and shot him three times. He was so big and heavy that the bullets didn't penetrate any of the vital organs. They just, you know, kinda' stuck in the flesh. Hank ran the Ducky Game with his wife. Technically, this made Hank a jointee rather than a ride guy. Usually, jointees were of a higher intellectual and social strata than ride guys. The Ducky Game, where Hank worked was a punk game where kids all won something. The ducks floated along a little water canal and a kid just picks up one to see what the prize is. Hank was the type of guy that would see a little handicapped girl with her parents and run out to give her a teddy bear. After the shooting, he straightened right out and there were no more beatings. In summary, Sally plugged him three times and didn't hit a vital organ. More people should do that. You wouldn't need all the trials and lawyers. He was with Steele's every year, a regular. That was the thing with Steele's that Buck always liked. There was such continuity. The same people came back to work year after year. There was always the hope that next year would be better than the last and a ride guy or even a jointee would straighten out.

Sterling Palmer came with Steele's from Missouri one summer, under a probation deal. It was in the '50s. He had stolen a horse. Not a car thief, but a horse thief. As fitting to Steele's tradition, they gave the guy a chance and he worked out pretty well. Buck figured that past performance was not a good indicator of future returns.

Not all of the ride guys turned out better than expected. There was an instance where this one former ride guy, Buck finally pieced some things together, James C., from a real outlaw family in Stoughton, Wisconsin, was hanging around the carnival during setup in East Gary, Indiana, as it was called at the time. A thunderstorm came up and James disappeared while Buck was working on a ride. When the thunderstorm was over, one window of the International (truck) had been broken out. Buck thought that was really weird because that guy James was up in the area for no reason. He'd left the show earlier in the year under some unpleasant circumstances. After setup and during the next show, in Freeport, Illinois, the 'tubs', the large round seats people ride in came off of the Octopus during a ride. Actually, they flew off the Octopus at a high rate of speed. Buck never told the insurance company any of this, of course, but there was a horrible storm that came up again when the carnival was playing Freeport. James C. had come back. The nuts on that tub were tampered with during the storm. Buck was sure the wacky bastard had loosened up those nuts just enough, so that when that ride started up, there were just a few threads to pull loose and *bang*. Luckily there were no serious injuries. Some dogs howl at the moon and some ride guys sabotage equipment during storms. These thunderstorms set this nut off and he damned near killed some people.

Back in Hillsboro it was time to perform the cash management function for the ride guys. This entailed giving cash advances of about seven bucks to each employee to get them through the day. None of these people had checking accounts, or even the legitimate I.D. to get a bank account. Some of them were working on being invisible to the IRS or ex-wives. Every day cash was handed out so the boys could get lunch, buy cigarettes and terrorize whatever little town they were in. They would also use the money to participate in any novel nonsense that was going on with the carnival. When the Bear Wrestling attraction came to the sideshow, the ride guys were some of its best customers.

" I'm thinking that I should run the guys short of cash before setup." Buck was musing to the other family management. "You see, if they don't have any money the day before, I don't have to haul them out of a pool of their own vomit, and I don't have to risk my life working setup with someone still bombed or just coming out of a coma. What do you think?"

Maytha said that the ride guys would just come to her trailer at some ungodly hour and ask for money. It was a lot like feeding a raccoon, they always come back.

"O.K., O.K...." Buck dumped the management idea. His mom was always right about these things. But then, she and Aunt Charlotte always were a little soft on the ride guys. They would do their laundry, and basically treat them like part of the family. In return though, the ride guys really acted like part of the family. They became a posse that escorted and protected the Steele kids both on and off the midway. They helped make what may have been an inherently dangerous place to raise kids, a very safe one. A hundred watchful eyes were following the kids wherever they went in the carnival. The younger Steele's often griped that they couldn't get away with anything. Instead of having one set of parents to answer to, they had three. Then they had the security service of every other carnival employee to contend with.

Another Ride Guy of note was called the Mortician. To call the guy a firebug or some kind of loony would be too simple. Burt was a grudge arsonist. Something would touch the guy off and he would torch your store. Something would hit him wrong and things would start to burn. Buck specialized in this type of employee. Some employers would lose this guy faster than having a malignant mole removed. The liability was too great. No business could risk having such a nut around. But Buck was always up for a twisted challenge. What would happen, say, if you kept the guy away from matches? How about getting him to stop smoking? Maybe keep him away from flammable cleaning fluids. This was manageable. Besides, sometimes it's hard to replace a ride guy. Burt was in.

Burt was started on the Dark Ride. It was a long trailer that opened up to form a spook house of sorts. Kids, also lovingly referred to as 'punks' in the carnival business, walked in one side of the trailer and moved through different scary scenes accompanied by music and sound effects. Things were going pretty well for a while. Burt got on the show in Rockford, Illinois and would travel the whole circuit.

Burt had just recently been a morgue attendant. Like most carnies, he had a nickname. His was "Mortician". So Burt, er, the Mortician started working the Dark Ride. Funny thing was that Burt also had a dark side. Dark Ride!

The Mortician had a hot temper and would let it get the better of him on occasion. Mad at the grocery store? Burn it down. Mad at the carnival? Burn down the Dark Ride.

Hygiene was an issue with Burt. This is not unknown with carnies, but Burt and Burt's girlfriend were both short on grace and long on smell. "He was dirty, repulsive, and smelled real bad—same for his girlfriend!" was the way it was put. But something about his background appealed to Buck.

Burt had a run in with the Dark Ride. This big spook-house trailer had a moveable section that swung out to increase the size of the experience. The Mortician was not paying close attention one time and the swinging section swung around and pinned him to the side of the ride. It would be immature to hold a grudge against an inanimate object, but if you're looking for maturity at a carnival, keep looking.

One day, late in the season, the last load of juniors exited the Dark Ride. Smoke was seen curling out of the roof vents. A great hubbub erupted and the fire was extinguished. No casualties reported, except one; the ride itself. Burt had reported the fire and helped in it's dousing. It looked suspicious enough for Buck to move him to the Tilt-A-Whirl. How much trouble could he get into there?

The carnival is not a good place for the accident-prone. On Burt's new job as operator of the Tilt-A-Whirl, he was the responsible party for dozens of little kids every run of the ride. You strap the little buggers into seats and tilt them up in the air and whip them around until they almost puke. Well, some of them do puke, and maybe this is what prompted the Mortician to take a break. Claiming to be overcome by carbon monoxide fumes, he called an ambulance to take him to an emergency room. Burt continued to spin kids until the ambulance arrived, walked over and climbed in for a ride to the hospital.

Steele's Amusements was in the business of making fun. But in a deeper sense, Buck Steele in particular was in the business of saving souls. Buck took the weird, the disadvantaged, and even the criminally disposed and tried to give them a direction. A job, money management, and some strict rules pulled some of these people out of the rut they were in and headed them on the straight and narrow. The Mortician was one of these guys. After leaving the carnival, he went with another show for a while. Then he started his own show of sorts as a Santa Claus. By all accounts the guy turned out really well. Nothing burned after Steele's Amusements.

The jointees or concessionaires were a different breed altogether. Unlike a ride guy or ride jock, jointees or agents were usually more educated and settled in a particular profession, lived in a home and some even paid taxes. Steele's had long term relationships with concessionaires and could count on them year after year. Take, for instance the Mouse Game operator:

Plywood, paint and mice. That's all you need to get set up in business. Most people are familiar with the Mouse Game. The fuzzy little critter is tossed onto the playing board and needs to scurry into one of the numbered or lettered holes along the edge. This sounds like something mice do naturally, go directly to a hole that is. Turns out that not all mice do this. Wild mice run into the first hole they see because they want to live. Lab mice or pet mice or pet store mice are not as obliging. Through selective breeding, lab mice have lost their instinct to hide, and that's why the Mouse Game operator knows to procure mice at a nearby farm. Wild mice.

The idea that the Mouse Game can be rigged is counterintuitive. Some have said that placing a drop of ammonia or vinegar on the hole the jointee wants the mouse to go down will attract him, the male mouse to go there. This almost sounds scientific. Male mice are supposed to believe that girl mice smell like ammonia. Is this game reliant on mouse romance? But why would the joint agent want the mouse to go down a predicable hole? Any observer for a few minutes could see the pattern and bet on the right hole. The agent would lose his shirt or whatever he is offering at the time. No, this game is not rigged. Almost any attempt at 'gaffing' the Mouse Game would backfire. The joint agent would go home broke and ashamed.

One of the few actual success factors that the Mouse Game guy *can* manipulate are related to the speed of the game. Fast mice are best. The more times you can run the game the more money you can make. So, an indecisive or even lazy mouse cannot last long in this business. The joint agent will quickly decide if a certain mouse is a performer and cull him from the herd if he or she is not.

10-in-1

Everyone at Steele's was elated. This was a major coup. Percilla, the Monkey Girl was going to be with the carnival for one or two seasons. Percilla was a big-time act. She had been with Ringling Brother's Circus and was one of the classics of the sideshow business. Why she was the Monkey *Girl* at the age of thirty-something was a bit of a mystery, but Steele's had her and she was a big draw.

Your typical Monkey Person has the genetic disorder called hypertrichosis or hirsutism. This allows for, in the best of cases, hair to cover just about every visible part of the body; serious, black, thick, steel wool type hair. Individuals blessed with this genetic makeup have their choice of jobs: Monkey Girl, Monkey Woman, Wolf Boy, Wolf Man, the possibilities are only limited by the imagination. And now, Steele's Amusements had her and her husband, Emmett the Alligator Man.

Buck had already assumed that he would not have the services of Percilla's husband. The Alligator Man had decided to step into a managerial roll as Percilla's talker. After all, Emmett knew the whole history of the Monkey Girl and was the best one around to promote her in the business at hand. Also, some had suggested that the Alligator Man's own condition amounted to nothing more than a serious case of scaly skin and therefore, not worth a significant admission cost. Call it semi-retirement, but Emmett would bark the talk, create the tip, and bring customers into the 10-in-1 to see his lovely wife, Percilla, The Monkey Girl.

The 10-in-1 was shaping up nicely. Well, at Steele's, it was more like a 4-in-1. The traditional ten acts shown for one admission price were shortened due to lack of available talent. Also, unless the act was a huge draw, Steele's would rather use the space for a ride or two. Rides make money. The sideshow acts could also make money, but they were independent contractors and managed their own funds. Buck had to trust them to report an accurate ticket sales count and pay their 'privilege' or percentage. This amounted to 25% of sales, but if the sideshow had a problem counting, and say, *missed a few*, it could amount to a net loss for

Steele's. Sideshow acts had to be chosen very carefully.

Suicide Simon was also coming into the show. Buck wanted to talk to Suicide and get some of the particulars of his act. This was an important vetting process. Suicide Simon had to convince Steele's that he could blow himself up profitably each night of the run and make money.

Buck headed from Maytha's Headquarters trailer to the sideshow area. Suicide and his assistant and barker were just unloading their setup. This was an interesting concept quite new to Steele's Amusements. Not unlike the human cannonball show, this dynamite trick could be a winner.

"So I hear they call you Suicide Simon?" Buck asked as he extended his hand.

"Huh? Oh. That's right, Buck." Suicide said as he adjusted his external hearing aid amplifier. "I get called some other things from time to time too, but Suicide is just fine. You get my contract ready?"

"Sure, it's the standard boiler plate we use. Your privilege is 25% payable each night until teardown. Tell me how this works."

"What?" Suicide was as deaf as a post, so Buck repeated the question.

"Oh, yeah. I set up the stand and run through one box per show. Two shows each night. Jimmy here does the talkin' for me and we create quite a fuss. The whole thing is centered on the explosion. We get the expectations built up real high and then blow those folks' minds."

"Let me get this straight. After Jimmy gets the tickets sold during the afternoon, you get into this casket with a stick of dynamite, close the lid and set the explosive off?" Buck was starting to consider the consequences of such a trick.

"That's about the size of it. We gotta do a pretty big build-up job because the climax is sorta' short and violent. The tip usually hangs around for a while and helps the grab joints with sales. People get hungry waiting for a show like this. Maybe it's blood lust."

"How dangerous is this for the ticket holders? I mean, have you ever had any problem containing the debris flying all over?"

"What? Dangerous? Every once in a while we blow some hardware where it shouldn't go, but on the whole, this is fairly safe. The box gets blown to Hell, but see, this wood that the box is made of? It's just lightweight pine. It puts on a good show but usually doesn't go too far."

"O.K. but you have to put up some kind of net. I mean, our

insurance is a big enough problem." Buck explained. "You *have* to have some safety barrier to contain anything, er, dangerous."

"Yeah, we can do something like that, but you don't have anything to worry about. I been doin' this for years.

Suicide would climb into a wooden coffin and explode a stick of dynamite inside, blowing him and the wooden box to smithereens. Actually, Suicide Simon never lost any body parts, just his hearing in both ears and some cuts and bruises. The coffin itself would go flying in pieces everywhere and was a general danger and nuisance, not a bad gimmick, just a liability nightmare. He used real, honest-to-God dynamite and the explosion would be heard for miles around. You just couldn't tell the difference between that explosion and some other real problem like a ride blowing up or a terrorist event.

"So Suicide, if I can call you that, do you, like, blow any blood or anything into the crowd when the blast happens?"

"Sure! That's the best part! This really gets the kids going when they feel the spray of real body fluids wafting over them. It's realism. I'm known for my realism. I *have* thought of using a bag of fake blood to add to the experience, but it don't just seem right. So whatever hits 'em during the show is real me. This is better than anything Disney World can do. And now, you can have it here too. Honest, this show has the benefit of years of consumer research!"

"Christ Simon! You mean to tell me that you spew blood over the whole crowd twice every night and it's not fake?" Buck was not exactly believing this.

"The thing is," Simon said, "I gotta do something nobody else has thought of. You might say I have put myself into this show wholeheartedly. A few scratches per show don't amount to much."

"O.K., I'll come to the first show and see how this works out. Make sure you put that net up." Buck was satisfied that this was edgy, but worth the risk. When the word got out about this crazy son-of-a-bitch, people would come from miles around to see the pyrotechnics.

Percilla The Monkey Girl seemed to be quite the tame act compared to Simon the human bomb. How much trouble could she be? Emmett the Alligator guy would seem more like a museum curator in comparison to the weird shit about to grace the midway at Steele's. Bring it on.

The next act to display in the 10 or 4-in-1 was a kid that Buck called the Foot Doctor. The act was comprised of a 15-year-old black kid that had no arms. But what this kid was missing in eye-*hand* coordination he more than made up for in eye-*foot*. He could do anything with his toes! He could do surgery with his feet if needed. He could thread a needle, work scissors, and even snap his toes just like you would snap your fingers. Buck took the kid out to a small lake in Stoughton, Wisconsin fishing just to check out his pedal dexterity. Jesus! Baits the hook with his feet. This is pretty interesting, but hard to tell how good the draw will be.

"Hey, Doc." Buck was casting his line. "Can you handle a beer *and* the fishing rod?" Buck figured that if the kid could get by on his own at fifteen he might as well drink beer.

"Ah sure can. Set 'er right there and ah'll grab it." The Foot Doctor motioned his direction with a nod. "No sense in fishin' if you can't drink beer at the same time. 'Sides, I use the bottle as a kickstand. It steadies me."

Buck popped the top off a longneck and placed it within foot reach of the Doctor. "What does your talk sound like? Do you tell people about why you're missing limbs?"

"Nope, I don't git into that. That just bores people anyways. I more talk about what I can do wiff ma feet. F'rinstance, I write letters, lick the envelopes an' address 'em. Usually I can get all my bidness done during the show. Then ah comb my har, brush ma teeth 'n all. They really like to see me thread a needle and sew stuff. Ah try to keep it mixed up so the act isn't gettin' stale."

After a few hours and a dozen bluegill Buck and the Doc returned to the midway. Things were set and it was time to open up.

As they rolled up near the generator trucks, Buck spotted Emmett the Alligator Man waving him over. Hoping there was nothing wrong with his prize act, Buck jogged over to see what was up. Emmett was smiling a big dizzy smile, like usual.

"Mr. Steele, why don't you come over and talk to me and Percilla for a while..." Emmett was somewhat plastered, which explains the stupid smile on his face. Good-natured guy, though. "Sure, Emmett, be right over after I park the armless kid and see to a few things. Buck moved toward the show trailer where the Wild Woman Gorilla Show was held. The Foot Doctor would have to tack his act onto the spot right before the finale fright, the Gorilla Show. The Gorilla was one of those illusion things where this Wild Woman magically transforms, "right before your very eyes" into a raging gorilla. You have to be kinda stupid to buy into the whole premise, but the kids like the thing. It makes a lot of racket. Hell, anything will work if it makes enough noise. This gorilla act is done with some projectors and lenses. You start with the

Woman, a few lens changes, and presto, loud ape. The hook is that the Woman is a very beautiful, 22-year old Midwestern girl. A real stunner. The expectation is that this calm, demure little gal will transform into something unlike what you see in the beginning. The whole show relies on the Woman transforming and going, literally *ape shit* on the audience and creating havoc. In one typical show, the hype is built up so well that a stampede is created as the crowd blows off from the tent. Once, several white shirted Civil Defense officers, monitoring the show for crowd control were knocked down as the crowd surged out of the tent, evidenced by dusty footprints covering the back of their crisp white shirts. It was of historical interest that the Civil Defense had lost some relevance in the post war period and, in this case decided to protect carnival patrons rather than America from Soviet invasion. In another instance, the Civil Defense, still wearing WWI era helmets assisted cotton-candy users if they were stung by the ubiquitous bees. For the upside, it only takes up about 10 feet of the trailer, so there is plenty of room for the Foot Doc to answer his mail and sew his socks.

    Maytha, Buck's mom held down the office trailer and had some paperwork for Buck to tend to. This was the H.Q. and the nerve center of the carnival. It was where the money is kept.

Buck heard the explosion, not just a sharp bang, but a crushing, heart stopping Whumph! It was followed by the roar of flying debris and screaming people. At first no one recognized what had happened. It was a shock. Then Buck's memory returned and allowed him to recognize that the horrific explosion was Suicide Simon's act. Something must have gone very, very, wrong. People were screaming and running in all directions from the epicenter, Simons' trailer.

Ray and Vinnie both ran flat out to the scene to aid the survivors. Buck was hot on their heels. The place was a mess with shards of wood scattered everywhere. Standing in the middle of the chaos was Suicide Simon, bowing grandly and throwing his arms in the air. Suicide was shouting, "Thank-you, thank-you", but nobody was paying attention. All the ticket holders were running for their lives and the children were crying. Smoke filled the trailer and far out into the seating area. No flames were visible though, so Buck, Vinnie and Ray stopped and looked around to see what needed to be done.

Ray said, "If this is how this act goes, we have to stop it now. People on the Ferris Wheel are screaming and think they're all gonna die." Vinnie agreed and walked over to talk to Suicide.

Buck surveyed the damage and decided that he better talk

to the sheriff's deputy just arriving.

"Are you the management here." The officer was obviously excited and shook up.

"Yes, I'm one of the *survivors*. We have a handle on this and nobody is hurt. Has there been any complaints?" Buck was trying to calm the cop down.

"Are you kiddin'? This blast was heard all over the county. We have six people at the gate wanting ambulance service. They say their ears are ringing or damaged or something."

Buck tried to lighten the mood. "Always some people whinin' about something. They all knew this show was loud and they still plunked down their money. Don't worry about a thing. We'll calm things down. Boy that Simon really puts on a show, huh? Maybe we should raise the ticket prices some. You see any press here? You can't buy better advertising than word of mouth and the press!" Buck was elated at the general reaction of the crowd, but a little worried that Suicide had overdone it a mite. It was too soon to evaluate the cost/benefit ratio of this act. We would have to see how many people actually make it to the emergency room and if they wanted to sue. This really was an impressive show. Maybe we could offer the victims or customers some free rides. The cops were for the moment mollified, but that may not last long.

Suicide Simon was wiping blood from a vicious cut on his ear when Buck approached him. "What the hell is this? We didn't buy into this mayhem!" Buck was apoplectic. He had a panic stampede at the main gate and some really pissed off cops to deal with. Simon was smiling, showing his bleeding gums. "Pretty dramatic act, huh?" Simon ran his tongue over red tinged teeth. "We gonna set up again for the 10 o'clock. You oughta' be here for that one."

"I told you to put up a net and catch all this flying crap. We have a dozen people swearing they'll sue us." Buck was pumping out hyperbole. "Are you insane?"

"What? I have a little concussion hearing loss after a show. Can you repeat that?" Simon was wagging his head from side to side.

"You dim wit! Clean this mess up and bring us your gate. We have to figure if the income is worth this hassle." Buck spun and headed to the entry area to survey the human damage. A few people were gathered at the carnival entrance debating whether to head for the county hospital. Buck edged in and adopted the concerned parent stance. "You guys all right? Man, that explosion was intense! We had no idea that *independent show* was so loud. I wouldn't blame you if you took that guy to the cleaners, but it would be a short ride. He isn't affiliated with this carnival, and I don't think he has any assets to speak of. And besides, he *does* advertise the act as being shocking, high energy and able to blow you away." It seemed none of the customers were keen on going to the hospital if it wasn't necessary. "If any of you are coming back tomorrow, I'd like you to be my guest on the midway." Buck was handing out stacks of Steele's Amusements complimentary ticket books as he spoke. After schmoozing the rattled customers, Buck headed back to the HQ trailer to decompress.

Maytha and the others were nowhere in sight but were probably working damage control on the midway. Ray came in the office trailer a few minutes later. "This bomb guy has gotta go. I'm not gonna cover for him if he gets anyone hurt with his wacky show."

"I know what you mean. The sheriff's deputy was all out of sorts about it. We may not be able to contain them if this continues," Buck said.

Crap, Emmett the Alligator Man wanted Buck to stop by their trailer an hour ago. Better check out the headline act before something else goes wrong.

"How's it goin'?" Buck ducked in the Monkey Girl's

trailer.

"C'mon in." Emmett slurred.

"Been a little busy, Emmett." Buck said. "Sorry I'm late. How are you two doing?"

"Honey!" Emmett yelled back into the trailer. "We got company!" Percilla the Monkey Girl showed up just fastening her costume. Emmett said, "Do you know my wife Percilla? She's a lovely girl…"

"Yes, of course, Hi, Percilla." Buck said. Buck had met Percilla several times in just this way, but he rolled along with Emmett's boozy memory loss. If you go with the idea that people really say what they think when half in the bag, then Emmitt truly did see Percilla as lovely and still a girl. There is a mate for everyone on Earth. Emmett and Percilla are the living proof of that. "What do you think of the show so far Percilla? As advertised?"

"Oh, yes!" Percilla was the most mild mannered of people. "We like the towns up here. The people are so nice to us. We should work with your show next year too…"

Wham! Another violent explosion followed by the whoosh of flying debris. This time Buck immediately recognized the sound and headed out to the show area. Simon's second show.

Looking down the midway, Buck could see the cops already on the scene. Jesus, they wouldn't go for this much longer. Buck's jaw hurt from gritting his teeth.

Suicide Simon's set looked much like the eight o'clock show, wood pieces everywhere, Suicide standing in the middle, in tatters with a gash on his forehead.

"Look, Simon..." Buck started up. "We can't let this go on. This is a residential area and the cops are wound tight about the noise. Any crowd that you attract is just being scared off the other end. And to tell you the truth, I don't think this is safe. In fact, you loony bastard, I don't want to see you kill yourself in front of a lot of kids here. I think tonight was your last show." It had dawned on Buck that this show could spawn all sorts of litigation. The sound was so loud that it couldn't help but attract witnesses. Only a matter of time before some enterprising attorney gathered up a few shell-shocked customers and got the personal injury ball rolling. In fact, who is to say that this crazy Simon doesn't have *plants* in the audience just waiting to shake down Steele's or the insurance company? That's it! No wonder this Simon fellow doesn't have anything. He could be in on a very clever scam. He travels with his own secret set of plaintiffs! Genius. Pure genius.

Flat Joints and Gaff Stores

'Gaffing' a game is the carnival equivalent of tinkering with the win setting on a casino slot machine. The carny operator has different parameters that can be adjusted to insure a profit for him and, on occasion, a PR win for one of the customers. Much is made about the honesty of carnival games. Just as in real life, honesty is a relative matter. The odds of winning any carnival game are dependent on a set of variables. Some of these variables are controlled by the player of the game and some controlled by the wicked, dishonest slimy carny behind the counter. Also, some of these variables are controlled by Mother Nature, or God. To hear the law enforcement authorities tell it, all is well if Mother Nature, God, or a customer fools with the game settings. It is not

O.K. if the agent (carny) fools with the game settings. What on Earth is the difference between the local Indian casino adjusting a slot machine pay-out or a carny doing the same thing? None. But fortunes in tax money have been squandered by police investigating carnival games. It is important for them to save you from blowing $2.00 on a gaffed (rigged) game, yet you willingly pay a magician to trick you for entertainment. It all comes down to your version of reality. Do you want to go to the carnival all defensive and worried about being cheated? Or would it be better to go to the carnival and think like the audience member in a magic show. "Gee, how does that carny do that?" Mental health is improved if you live life with the latter attitude. The carny needs to feed his kids, pet snake, or whatever. He is trying to play a trick on you for very small stakes. Have fun with that.

So, what games are gaffed? All of them, you idiot! All of them if you believe that gaffing is anything that lessons your chance of winning. Even the games where every player wins, like the Ducky Game, are rigged to allow the carny to make money. The prizes are worth less than the cost of the ticket to play. This is capitalism. The level of 'gaff' is what gets people all cranked up. If the carny shows some real 'flash', or in normal-speak places some very extravagant prizes in view, gets your expectations up and then makes it impossible for you to win, you are really mad. Some boneheads even call the cops. It is fun to imagine the complaint: "Sir, this filthy carny cheated me out of my rent money. I played the basketball throw for three days and never won a Teddy Bear. Then I noticed that the basketball rim was bent. Bastard!" Obviously the local Special Agent in Charge of the FBI should be called in. J. Edgar Hoover was the patron saint of morons. (at least until 1972 he was)

It is difficult to get a carny to admit gaffing a game. They are very defensive about it. It sounds a little dirty. But most games on the midway have tricks to them and a carny does not believe a game to be gaffed unless it is really, really impossible to win. If a game can be won once in one thousand tries, most carnies consider it to be a fair deal. After all, look at that 19-inch color TV you could win!

At Steele's Amusements the games were by and large honest. Very dull you say? Remember that this is entertainment. Remember that the Steele's made money and supported kids, paid for law school, engineering college, land and fun. One way to encourage repeat business, both from individuals and fair boards is to run a fun midway with a reasonable chance to win.

Some of the 'flat' stores had interesting characteristics. A 'flat' store is a game booth where the game is gaffed or rigged. The more innocent the game, the more possibility for it to be gaffed.

Take that Dart Game where you pop balloons in a prescribed pattern with darts to win prizes; pretty straight forward is the general consensus. You throw these darts at the balloons, pop enough and win the Teddy Bear or whatever. Government and Science enter the picture and things get a little more complicated.

Buck's mom, Maytha was in charge of the Dart Game for quite a while. She would inflate balloons and tie them off until her fingers bled. Since the players of this game would puncture many balloons, the need for rapid inflation was great. There was no one more honest than Buck's mom. After all, how deceptive can blowing up balloons get?

In the quest for regulation of this industry, the states would send out inspectors to monitor the midway games. In fact, the Dart Game was under federal *and* state scrutiny. It seems that there is an optimal pressure a balloon must be inflated to in order for the average dart to penetrate it and the game to be deemed honest. Here is where carny corruption can enter. If the balloon is under-inflated, the dart may just bounce off, cheating the player out of a valuable prize. Throngs of unknowing 'marks' can be defrauded in this way. Could there be any other reason for under-inflation? Obviously, the lung capacity of the game operator could be a factor, but this is an area ripe for regulatory oversight.

"Hey, I wanna see some *shine* on those balloons, ma'am! The inspector would say as he thumbed through his idiot manual. A shiny balloon is a properly inflated balloon. If they are dull looking, look out. Also, the inspector may look for a point on the dart. If the dart has a blunt point, the balloon won't pop even if you hit it, even if it is shiny, and even if you throw it very hard. Judging by the hundreds of balloons that Maytha or her helpers had to replace in a day, their game was scrupulously honest to the point of a give-away.

Have you ever noticed a pack of Lucky Strike cigarettes? That familiar 'bull's eye' on the pack is the preferred graphic for thousands of carny games worldwide. The easily recognizable logo is eye catching and tends to attract marks to an entertaining carnival game. The idea of the game is to toss a nickel onto the Lucky Strike board and hope that it lands fully within the circle of the small bull's eye. This sounds simple? Well, if you are a degenerate smoker and ultra-familiar with the exact dimensions of the Lucky Strike logo, you might notice that one side of the game board has smaller bull's eyes than the other. In fact you might even notice that the words Lucky Strike don't appear on the game board, just the circles. If during the course of the day, the agent running the game is losing too much merchandise, he may just flip the board to improve his odds a bit. Can the game still be won? Sure. Is this honest? Sure, because who is to say that the larger circles aren't *too* large? Is this game gaffed? No. You can still win it and with practice can improve your chances. Simply the win percentages have been adjusted to stay in pace with business conditions. If this makes you mad, then go play basketball with a bent rim.

Inspector

They showed up in very, very plain cars. Only two types of people that drive stuff like that, religious fundamentalists and undercover cops. These two Fords contained the latter, and from the parking area, the stiffs were seen squeezing between the Tilt-A-Whirl and the generator trucks. Armed with little tiny scales, rulers, note pads, and badges, they spun right and marched down the midway straight for the joints. They didn't want to be seen so soon, but the jointees were on the lookout for them already. Buck heard of the incursion and took the same heading.

From the feds all the way down to the county and local police, these coppers all had the same lecture, goes something like: "Don't fraternize with the carnies! Don't be their friend. If they think you are not in complete control they will walk all over you.

Start with showing who's boss. Crack the most likely crooked game first and fast. Get them all buzzing about how tough you are. Once you get the joints inspected, lax up, tell the uniform guys what is going on and leave. The uniforms will ride on the carnies until the show's over. Make sure the uniforms patrol the parking lots. All the drug dealing will start there and move inward, to the trailers. And for God's sake, watch the perimeter fences. Booze and dope will flow through the perimeter unless you are on it like flies on shit. Make sure the officers are in body armor at all times. You never know when something will cut loose. Keep warning of pick pockets on the midway and pay special attention to teenagers near the big rides. That's where the alcohol and drugs move. Remember that there are similarities between all carnies: They're clannish and do not trust outsiders. Many of them are running from something and have a need for unaccounted for cash income. Figure that most of them are dodging child support payments, check garnishments, the IRS and the like. Some of these carnies are born in the business, with families involved for generations. Some of them are stray dogs that have just wandered into the life; they come and go. A lot of these carny types think cops are stupid and they disdain you. Some of them have a real respect for the law. How you tell them apart is a mystery. These guys can talk the pants off a nun so you gotta take everything they say with a healthy dose of skepticism. Many carnies are tough guys and approach problem solving by kicking someone's ass. They can try this with the police as well. Carnies will do anything to keep their employees out of jail. They will hide information, and generally hinder your efforts. They will obstruct, obfuscate and sideline the truth."

"You cannot and I repeat, CANNOT plan for a carnival on the day all the stuff arrives. Weeks ahead of time you have to make a layout of the grounds, and set up a deployment schedule. You gotta cover the office trailer with at least one uniform because they handle a ton of cash in there. One officer has to be available each night at closing to escort the manager to a bank night deposit slot. You need to set up and monitor a first aid station. Make sure that you have access to the PA system and an area to corral lost kids. Be on the lookout for the usual gang types marching through the area. They like to be seen, so make sure you see them and they see you. Make a presence. The more the carnies and crooks see you the less trouble you will have."

The undercover cops are dressed kind of casual for work, Buck noticed. Part of this inspection gig is fun though, so they dress accordingly. Buck makes it to the Dart Game just as Officer

#1 pulls out his inspection manual.

"Well, gentlemen, if I knew you were coming I would have whipped up some hot dogs and coke. At any rate, I am glad you are here and am ready to help you." Buck smiled as he recognized one of the policemen, a county cop he had met before.

"And you are…" The leader of the pack asked.

"My name is Al Steele, the owner of Steele's Amusements. My friends call me Buck. Heck, even my mom calls me Buck. Sometimes Buckie. You guys have any particular joints to check out or just the usual shake down?"

"Mr. Steele, we just need to check out all the games tonight. We already have had a complaint from a patron that some games could be gaffed. (The copper was *insinuating* the games could be rigged. He used the carny term 'gaffed') We figure if we start off on a good note, we can all relax here. I figured we would start at one end and move through the whole lot. Any objections?" Officer #1 was not expecting to hear any objections.

"Of course not." Buck said. "I'll just tag along if that's O.K. with you. Maybe we can fix you up with lunch at the cookhouse in a few minutes."

"Buck," the copper was getting with it, "this may take a while. We're gonna fine-tooth this midway to make sure we're covered."

Sidling up to the Dart Game, Officer #1, named Dinkins, asks the jointee running the game what the price per dart is. Wants to see if the guy knows without looking at the sign. The carny says three for a quarter. Cop wants to see the darts and checks to see if they have points on 'em. They do, sort of, so he asks what the prizes are and how they are scored. Small, medium and large balloons? They all look pretty much the same. "So how is some kid supposed to know which balloons are the small ones when he wants the big prize? I mean, I can't tell them apart, can you?"

The carny shrugs and said something lame like; "Kids are smarter than you think…"

"What is the trade-up policy. If a player wins X number of little things, what can he trade them in for?" If the player gets six small balloons popped, he can trade the six little plastic dolls for one larger crummy stuffed animal. Sounds like a legit, but typically bad deal. What the Hell.

"So officer, things pretty slow tonight? It seems that you guys are expending a lot of enforcement talent that might be used to pinch some felons or bank robbers, rapists?" Buck was working on a point. This was immediately lost by law enforcement.

"We think that the 'felons' might just be right here tonight.

In fact, we have a bench warrant out on a child support scofflaw we hope to find."

Buck popped up, "Lemme know who the guy is and I will personally bring him over. We don't like to hear of our guys avoiding their responsibilities. Certainly not *those* responsibilities anyway." Buck personally knew several of his employees that haven't filed tax returns this decade, but that was a federal thing. These cops wouldn't be concerned with that.

The fun police walked over to the Milk Bottle Game. Everybody knows how this one works: The Player throws a rubber ball at a stack of 5 usually aluminum white painted milk bottles. Three bottles on the bottom and two on top, in this case. The deal is the bottom bottles are weighted to make them a little harder to knock over. Officer Dinkins asked for, then took a ball and heaved it with all of his might at a bottle setup. Missed. Tried another. Missed. Officer #2 of the team picked up a ball, left-handed and slung it toward the bottle pyramid. Bang. The ball hit directly on the bottom bottles but nothing moved. In fact, the ball bounced right back so high the carny snatched it out of the air.

"Are those bottles nailed down or something?" The officer sounded a little testy.

Buck, sensing a problem, spoke up. "Neat trick! I don't

know how you did that, but you could have a job here in a minute! It *looked* like you really threw that ball hard, yet it didn't do anything. That is amazing. Here." Buck handed another ball to the carny behind the counter. The carny or jointee heaved the ball at the milk bottles and they all flew off the platform. "Strike!" Buck shouted. The ball then fell heavily into the catch net in back of the bottle setup. Buck offered the alibi: "I think you just needed to get a little more *English* on that thing, sir. This game is simple but takes a lot of practice. I used to be pretty good at this game when I was a kid, but now I'm real rusty. Some of these little-leaguer types around here really take us to the cleaners. Born pitchers, some of them. Maybe we should put a limit on how many big prizes they can walk away with...." Buck was noticing that Dinkins, the cop, was pulling out a small set of scales from its case. Here we go.

"Let's see those bottles for a minute," Dinkins indicated the milk bottles, and the jointee glanced at Buck for direction. Buck just blinked at him, resigned. The carny leaned behind the bottle platform and pulled up five bottles stuck on the ends of his fingers. They all watched as Dinkins weighed each one on his small scale. They all weighed exactly the same. The carny could have grabbed all 'light' bottles from behind the platform, Dinkins thought. This was not worth the time it was taking. Best move on.

Next the police worked a Bumper Joint that checked out O.K. and then the Glass Pitch. Officer #2, or Bradley, the man with the golden arm tossed a handful of coins, one at a time at the glass plates in the center of the booth. Each coin skidded off the plate and into the catch. Bradley asked, "Can we see if you are waxing the top of those plates? It seems like coins are sliding off them pretty easy and…"

Buck interrupted, "We hear that one a lot. When you think of it, wax would just slow the coin down. The agent running the joint would be kinda stupid to rig the game against himself. "Here." Buck motioned the carny to bring up a plate. "Feel it for yourself. Well, maybe a little dust, but nothing to affect the game."

It seemed each carny was ready, waiting and all the games seemed clean. Maybe a hot dog was the only thing the cops could get this time around. "Buck, why don't we take a break and check out that cookhouse…" Dinkins was temporarily disarmed. The other team of officers looked like they were getting nowhere fast and looked bored, wanting to leave.

The joint task force or whatever the hell it was called decided that 30 more minutes was more than they could stand. Both teams left quietly and Steele's Amusements resumed normal operation. The day was still young.

"The guy had a fake mustache, honest!" The agent running the Six-Cat told Buck.

"Yeah, I know, I saw him too. At first I thought it was one of our guys screwing around. Hell, they're always doing that. But then I saw that this wasn't one of ours at all, just that wise-assed inspector from Portage (Wisconsin)." Buck went on, grinning. "The guy must be making a career out of haunting carny joints just to find the 'G' (gaffed or rigged game)." Buck was incredulous. After all, the stakes here are small. There must be a way to neutralize this inspector before he gums up the works.

"How are you doing? My name is Al Steele, er, Buck. I am the general manager of this carnival." Buck looked square at the fake-mustachioed inspector. "You look like some kind of undercover type or something? We should talk. I think I have a proposition that you might like. You see, the State of Illinois, Hell, Wisconsin too for that matter, wants us to hire our own inspectors to pre-check all the rides and game joints. You know, make sure all the cotter pins are in the ride seats so the precious little ones don't fall out. Also, the state wants to be sure all the games are at least winnable. It seems some whiners run to the cops every time they fail to impress their girlfriend at the Pepsi-Ring Game.

Whad'ya think? Could you stand to make, say, ten bucks a game or ride to keep things straight here?"

Stan Stiglitz, with the fake mustache replied, "Well, the county hasn't authorized any overtime for this job anyway, so as long as this fits within state guidelines, I think it would be a good idea. This go for your other shows around here too?" Stan was warming to the concept of being an independent contractor.

"Absolutely." Buck popped. "We could use you from here all the way up to Green Bay! And, uh, you can leave the hairy lip thing at home unless you just like the way it looks." Buck finalized the contract.

Mean Streets Stoughton, Wisconsin 1972

The rumor was always out there, fueled by the ever-present carny paranoia gene. The carnival would be set up for the usual week's run, but toward the end, maybe even the last or slough day, townspeople will invade the midway and reek revenge. Buck always wondered why townspeople would come to the carnival during the week and then cause trouble at the end, but this was Stoughton, and it had it's own reputation. Like much of Wisconsin, the landscape had been scoured by ancient glaciers and heaped up into rocky hills all over the place. So once you have hills it follows that you have hill people, and Buck figured that this was part of the problem. Hill people enjoy a certain amount of seclusion and isolation from society and maybe this was the source of

Stoughton's suspicion about the carnival. These carny outsiders are up to no good. They want our women. They are dishonest. The word heard on the streets of Stoughton was, "They're comin' to getcha."

"You know, we might have a little problem," Buck was hearing from his ride foreman. "These yahoos want to mess us up this week." Slick had heard this talk at the local bar. Slick was, if nothing, the covert intelligence arm of Steele's Amusements. If you could hear it in a bar, he was on top of things.

"We always hear that. Doesn't matter where we go, somebody always tells us that trouble is coming. We can handle it, but make sure the ride boys don't do anything to set the marks off." Buck was in his live and let live mood. Community relations were always a little tricky in southern Wisconsin. He had to think about his crew as they crossed the Cheddar Curtain from Illinois into Wisconsin. OK, which one of the ride guys is dodging child support and where was the warrant issued? Same thing worked in the reverse, if one of the guys was wanted in Illinois. You had to be careful about these things because several of the ride crew boys had a problematic past. It was a real pain if the coppers exercised a warrant just when you got set up for a spot. Steele's needed the guys more than the jail did. Why couldn't the cops just lock 'em up in the winter?

Stoughton was set up and things looked good. It was hot and sunny. It was a perfect day for the locals to enjoy the whole carnival experience, including indigestion and profuse sweat. Life was good. Until the fuzz showed up.

"You the manager around here?" The cop was making the usual friendly introduction in front of Steele's office trailer. "We gotta talk." Deadpan man.

Buck was wondering how the authorities always seemed to find him so fast. In reality he only spent a few minutes at a time in the office trailer. Uncanny how efficient they were when they wanted to be. "I guess that's me. What can I do you out of? We already have the Chief coming here every night to transport money, are you helping too?" Buck was playing it cool. This cop wasn't the 'helping out' kind. He was way too officious to be a friendly.

"Mr. Steele, we have an arrest warrant for Jimmy Sparta, one of your employees. It seems he is wanted for, among other things, failure to appear in court. There is a court order regarding child support that he has ignored and we need to get him. Assuming that he isn't right here, do you mind if we search the premises and your vehicles?" The copper was set. If Buck tried to dampen the man's enthusiasm with legal claptrap, it would lead nowhere. These guys would search every nook and cranny until they found the errant ride boy.

"Well, I don't see any reason why you can't poke around until you find Jimmy. I don't even know if he's still here. You know these guys sorta' come and go. For all I know they work more than one carnival at a time. They're really hard to keep track of, honestly, but go ahead and look." Buck was already thinking that it would be inconvenient to lose Jimmy just now. He was already running a ride boy or two short. Maybe it would be best to play some interference. "You know, if the bugger is anywhere, he'd be over by the Sky Diver. I think he would be running that if he were here..." This was a blatant misdirection. Jimmy was at the opposite end of the midway. Buck was buying time to figure things out.

"OK, Mr. Steele, we'll go get him, but if you see him before we do, he would be well advised to wait for us and cooperate."

"Oh, sure officer, I'll certainly let him know." Buck had become Eddie Haskell for a moment.

As the officer and his partner headed for the carnival's back-end and the ride area, Buck bolted for the front-end and parking area. Jimmy would be there and he needed a heads up. Come to think of it, he needed more than that. The kid was really in trouble and messing up the day.

"Hey, Whitey, you seen Jimmy S.?" Buck was referring to Slick by his pre-prison nickname. Slick was always called Whitey because of his white hair, but after going up the river for some trumped up offense, they shaved his head. Since then, his name was Slick.

"Yeah, he's by the generator helping Smitty lift something up. Whad'ya need?"

"I need to make him disappear before the cops do. Come with me." Buck motioned in the central direction of the generator trucks. The game was afoot.

"Naw, I can't do that" Jimmy whined. "Shit it's hot up there."

"The last I heard, they don't air-condition the jail here either, it's up you go or you go with the cops." Buck was pushing Jimmy toward the truck's cab. The plan was for Jimmy to climb up on the cab and then hoist himself on top of the semi-trailer. If he laid flat on the trailer top, no one would find him. There were just a few flaws with this plan:

Flaw one was that it was sunny summer day in southern Wisconsin and the trailer top was all metal. This was like a solar frying pan and Jimmy became the sizzling bacon. That'll teach him to pay his child support.

Flaw two was that although this was the best hiding place in the area, the kids riding the Ferris Wheel could still see him. All it would take as one junior G-man in the bunch to rat him out. Jimmy had to play the odds.

As luck would have it, the cops didn't hear Jimmy's whimpering from on top of the trailer and nobody riding the Ferris Wheel cared to comment. He was out of trouble for now, but his freedom would remain in jeopardy. Maybe his ex-wife would find solace in the fact that he had no shirt on and would certainly die of sunburn.

With that small crisis out of the way, Buck could turn his attention to other management functions. The carnival had a deal with the Chief of Police to transport the fair board's share of receipts each night to the board secretary. The fair board signed a contract each year with Steele's Amusements to provide the carnival midway for their fair and the board secretary was the local official designated to receive the money. This contracted amount was set at one thousand dollars per night, and the Chief insisted on taking the money over by himself. How much trouble could that be? A free police escort. Well, nothing is ever free.

Wednesday rolled around and the fair secretary called on Buck to complain. "The deal is for you to pay us one thousand dollars each night. We've only been getting nine hundred. Whoever you have counting out the money has been making mistakes most of the time." The secretary sounded a little miffed.

"Um, what do you mean by most of the time? How many days has the count been off?" Buck had a sinking feeling in his gut.

"Including last year?"

"You mean that you were missing money both this and last year on a daily basis? And you haven't mentioned this before? We

NEVER miss a count!" Buck strained to keep control.

"We never said anything because we thought that was all there was to the payment. Maybe some money fell out of the bag?" Great, the fair secretary was running an alibi past him.

"Look, we always wad up the bag around the money and hand it to the Chief of Police. Chief Clamp. He takes it to you. If it comes up short, either your counting is off or he is pinching. How much is it off each time?" Buck was going to get to the bottom of this.

"It is always off by one hundred dollars, exactly."

"OK, from now on we are going to send one of our guys over to deliver the money. We have to see how the hundred is being stolen. And, here's a tip for you:

Never, ever keep quiet about missing money. Always let us know right away." Buck would have to watch this. Someone was dipping into the cookie jar and laying the blame on his carnival. This could not stand.

Meanwhile back at the carnival now in progress, things were heating up. Some of the townspeople, mostly teenage boys were taunting the ride jocks and concessionaires during the day. Normally the carnies knew to ignore this, but after a while the particularly mean banter was fraying some nerves.

Then the news hit the midway that one of the carnival boys who was in town to buy some supplies got jumped by a handful of townies. The Stoughtonites were a little drunk and wanted to repel the invader. The carny kid got bruised up a bit. Buck figured that an out of sorts Norwegian was the cause of this trouble. They were the meanest. Southern Wisconsin also had it's share of Germans, Swedes, and Polish, but it was the Norwegians that always swung first. Hoping that he could keep a lid on things, Buck headed for the office trailer to check on receipts and their next stop. He couldn't get out of Stoughton soon enough.

"What do you mean sending some punk kid with the fair's money?" Chief of Police Clamp was spitting as he spoke in front of the office. Guess he'd heard about the new money delivery procedure.

Buck eyed Chief Clamp over and decided that his first estimate of the Chief was correct. He was a big, dumb son-of-bitch. "Well, Chief, maybe you heard about the accounting problem." The Chief just shook his head and slithered off. Buck wondered why he gave up so easily.

Inside the office trailer, Buck saw his wife Judy cranked all the way up to red. "Hey, Clamp left pretty fast, was he here for long before I got here?"

Judy nodded. "We had a chat. He was pretty mad about getting cut out of the loop. He said that if we didn't give him the money to deliver he would pick me up by my ears and shake me like a beagle dog. So I told him that if he lifted me high enough, I could kick him, um, well, kick him." Judy was trying to be modest but Buck knew how this went. His wife was Hell on wheels if you got her riled and the stupid cop had got her riled. The Chief must have weighed his options and decided to leave before there was more trouble.

"Good chat. Hope that crooked bastard stays gone." Buck was counting the minutes before they could leave Stoughton.

Well the minute of teardown came. The carnies all put on their slough clothes, the ones that were so worn and torn that they weren't good for anything else and started taking apart the rides and concession stands. Meanwhile, the bars in Stoughton were emptying out. Half of the town was just drunk enough to charge the carnival midway and mess things up. As the townspeople started to walk onto the midway area, the carnies took notice. This crazy town had been giving them crap all week and the carnies were fed up. Buck figured that his people should blow off some steam and scare the townies away. The ride boys, jointees and others started picking up pipes, wrenches and large pieces of wood. This was gonna be a brawl. Two sixteen year-old townie girls got real scared and started to run for the rent-a-cop that the fair board provided for security.

"Those carny people are crazy and are gonna kill us. You gotta do something!" The girls were pretty excited. In fact they were so excited that they couldn't explain why they were at the carnival after closing. The rent-a-cop unholstered his weapon.

The faux cop actually looked intimidating as judged by the total number of things hanging from his belt. He had all the usual stuff like cuffs, mace, nightstick, and gun holster. But in addition to those things he had a flashlight, knife sheath, three ammo pouches, and something that looked like a TV remote control. He looked ridiculous and he was really pumped up with adrenaline. The rent-a-cop leveled his revolver at an approaching group of ride boys. "You might get me, but I'll kill six of you!"

Buck walked up just in time. "Back to work boys." Buck clapped his hands and the ride boys dispersed, leaving the skinny rent-a-cop shaking with his gun. "You always so nervous? Buck quipped as he waved and went back to the teardown. Time to go. If they were ever welcome in Stoughton, they weren't now.

The Fair Board

At the intersection of carnydom and government lies the bureaucracy known as the fair board. The carnival's main source of business is placement at county and state fairs throughout the summer and it is the fair boards that control that process. A fair board contracts with the carnival to provide rides, games and entertainment for a percentage of their gross revenue. Also, the fair board charges the joint owners by the foot for frontage space on the midway. Big money changes hands in this process. Big money, local government contracts and human beings are three ingredients to a volatile mix. Every winter carnival owners and fair board members get together at meetings and conventions to hash out the following season's contracts. Too many carnivals, too few gigs result in some competition for deals. This Kabuki dance is an ongoing affair carried out at convention hotel suites, hospitality rooms, rest rooms, truck stops and elsewhere.

On occasion, a normally straightforward business negotiation takes a twist. Fair board managers kick their feet, hem and haw and look for a little something to sweeten the pot. This could be termed corruption if it were anywhere else but at a convention in Milwaukee, Wisconsin.

The Brown County, Wisconsin (think Green Bay) fair board guy said "Buck, we really like the cut of your jib. You guys always run a real clean outfit and we wanna offer you the contract this year. How 'bout I have my girl here rap out the papers on her machine and we can get this all set?"

Buck met up with the board secretary later, set the deal for a $50,000 week of rides and fun. The fair board would pull 37% off the top and also get $2.50 per foot of the concession spaces. A good week for Brown County, Wisconsin and a good week for Steele's Amusements. Done deal.

That particular summer was unremarkable in terms of set up in Brown County. Uncle Ray established the beachhead and ordered the vehicles, trailers, rides, concessions, and carnies onto the lot. The whole operation fitted together like a giant Chinese puzzle and Ray plugged it into the diesel-electric generators at the end. Lights on. It's show time.

The fair board secretary sent a minion to fetch Buck for an impromptu meeting. It seems that the deal was not *quite* done. Well, the contract *was* signed last fall and the provisions of the contract *were* clearly spelled out. The proper authorities executed the contract and Steele's Amusements *did* expend all effort to set up the midway. Hundreds of man-hours were already used to build the carnival from mud to done, but the fair board secretary just remembered that he wanted an extra $1500 for something. It seems that this sweating functionary had a side business that the carnivals were always asked to donate money to. No, this wasn't part of the Brown County operation, *per se*, but it was customary. "In fact, Buck," the secretary cooed, "nobody has ever had a contract for this fair without making the *donation*."

Being a carnival owner and trained lawyer, Buck sensed irregularity. This smacked of or smelled something like a solicitation for a bribe. Not in Green Bay you say? "Hell, you are NOT going to shake me down, you fat little bastard!" The concise legal terminology came pouring forth. "We signed the contract last fall and you didn't say a damn thing about any *extra charges*."

"Well, Buck," the lizard-like, combed-over official whispered, "you're gonna do a real good business this week. I think this can be, er, *absorbed* in your overhead."

"I'll cram my overhead up your ass. I made no allowance for skimming when we negotiated the contract. Do you read the Chicago Tribune, shit-head? I happen to have very friendly relations with the City Desk editor there. How would you like to find your picture on the front page next to some *other* criminal at arraignment? Listen, we just blew a wad of money and time getting set up. Rather than pay you a bribe I could have the boys break this whole thing down in six hours and leave. Your fair? Fucked. So what's it gonna be pin-dick?"

"Um, Buck, you don't seem to be *grateful* here about the opportunity you have. We'll just have to let this lay until another time. I really do have other things to attend to." With that the malodorous fair board secretary slid out of the area.

The rest of the day, and in fact, week went as per usual. No vicious looking accidents, no police busts on the midway, just a normal week of spinning kids and raking in joint money. The grab joints sold plenty of hot dogs and popcorn. The County of Brown would see a nice revenue stream from the fair and all the attendees would have a fond memory of sunburn and mosquito bites; Wisconsin at its best.

Monday breakdown had commenced in earnest when the

minion showed up again. "Mr. Steele, the secretary would like to see you." Buck saw this coming. Return of the slime ball. The little bastard hadn't spoken to him all week, so it figures that something sinister was in the works. Buck strode over to the fair board office to hear this out.

"Well, Buck, we think things went pretty well this week, despite your reluctance to, uh, support our various other projects. In light of that we don't think we can use your carnival at this fair in the future. Ever."

"You are under the assumption that you will live forever, or that we will be in this business forever," Buck started. "Neither situation is possible. So, gordo, I don't see this as any long-term problem. What may be a long-term problem for you, though, is that carnival owners talk. They talk to each other, to each other's employees, to the press, to local police and other fair boards." Buck was ticking off contacts in rapid fashion on his fingers. "So if you think that you win this little argument you are wrong. If you think that your little deal is your little secret, you are wrong again. Everyone in this county knows about this kickback shit or will by next week. They also will know about you buggering that assistant of yours and anything else we can come up with. So, chunky, have a nice summer."

In the big scheme of things, losing the Brown County spot was not an Earth shattering development. Didn't have it before, won't have it again. The good news was that the fair board secretary was eventually bounced out of his position. Buck never heard of the slug again. Almost.

The fair board secretary story picks up again further south. Buck explained it this way: "I'll tell you a story from 50 miles away from where I am right now. (Buck was speaking from Rhinelander, Wisconsin) Back in the early '60's the people up here were very much against the black people. But there were a lot of young black people up here that came to work the bean fields and pea fields because Libby and a couple of other companies did a lot of canning here. And I remember meeting one of them; a real neat guy by the name of Barry Cox, a Jamaican. Very well educated and a neat guy. Ernie Farrow used to have a ride crew come in from Mississippi, so he had people, some of them black people. And they started setting up the carnival. The fair board let us know that they could not allow these blacks, including Barry Cox to work here and the racist bastards wanted them out. Fast forward to the first week in January (of the following year), it was the Wisconsin Fair Board Meeting at the Schroeder Hotel in Milwaukee. The picture you didn't see was of a brothel being raided Sunday morning, where the same fair board was. That one is in the paper, if you go back far enough. The whole fair board was dismissed after that. It came out in the paper that there was a new fair board the following August. They had pictures of them coming out of the whorehouse. I think I might have seen a familiar face or two in that group."

Slim

She pulled up in a big Buick Electra, a deuce-'n-a-quarter, and flashed her lights twice. Not looking for sex, necessarily, just a long talk in the night with a real person; a carny person. A warm fifth of Southern Comfort was plugged into the center console and Bobby Vinton was playing on the 8-track. Midnight.

Slim Jim was just finishing up from a days' work on the midway and spotted the mass of Buick sheet metal. Unwashed, SJ cruised to the passenger-side door and climbed in.

She was a Chicago socialite. She sat on top of the 'A' list and was probably missing a major party to be here tonight, but this is where she wanted to be. No chewing gum magnate or political family could replace the strange comfort that existed here. Slim listened to all her troubles like he knew what they were about. This guy with the lack of hair and abundance of late night time just looked at her and listened. He was free until 7:00 AM. No plans.

She had a small package wrapped in foil paper, a gift of sorts, but an important one. She was bringing Slim a set of teeth. SJ had been in need of some choppers for quite a while, but the carny dental plan had a 100% deductible that he couldn't pay. So Hilary the Socialite had him fitted for dentures at a swank Chicago north side dental clinic and was now delivering the prescription. Uppers and lowers. A perfect fit Slim noted. Case of Dent-u-Creme included. How to repay this debt? Crack the Southern Comfort and work on that.

"Hey, you have any ice?" Hilary asked. "This stuff is pretty good on the rocks."

"You mean like your marriage?"

"Sure, like that. Go get some ice."

Slim jumped out and ran to the cookhouse trailer. Ice, cubed or crushed, available 24/7. Back at the Buick SJ did the setups. "Where you supposed to be tonight?"

"Party at alderman Stoners'. The mayor is going to be there. I was in charge of pumping him for the United Way drive."

"Sounds like a good time, but I'm glad you came here

instead. You know the difference between the Chicago City Council and a porcupine?" SJ was grinning, showing a bright new smile. "With the Council, the pricks are on the inside..."

"Very funny," Hilary said. "Hand me the bottle."

"Why you want to be with those people anyway?"

"I don't. I'm here. Shut up and hold your glass steady. So how was the crowd tonight? Anything happen?"

"Naw, jus' the usual. A few really fat ones wanted to ride together on the Ferris Wheel. We had to tell 'em that we needed to balance the load. That didn't go over too good. People don't see their ass as a load, exactly. So we gotta explain how to place 'em on the wheel so the thing doesn't run backwards on us, out of control. Some of the brake wheels are a little bald and we gotta watch how we load up the ride.

"How fat were they?" Hilary was getting curious.

"Like 300 pounds apiece. Times three of 'em. We test the seats higher than that, but things get a little weird when we put these gals opposite a 100-pound kid. Sometimes we can't get the wheel to turn on the upside, or if we do, it drops like a rock after the peak. I don't know how to tell 'em they're just too fat."

"How about letting them each take a separate seat? And, also, make a big deal that they will get an extra turn because of the balancing act." Hilary said.

"Yeah, that could work. You ought'a be with us on the circuit. So, what's it like at home," Slim asked.

"Lyric Opera is constantly asking for money, sponsorships and advertising. Operation Push is pushing us around and Cook County Hospital is forming a new building authority that our banks need to be involved with. Never marry a bank president. Everybody wants a piece of your action. Home is hell."

"I bet everybody *does* want a piece of your action." Slim started to draw out his deep Southern accent. "But you come to see me anyway. Ma'am, I'm honored." SJ leaned over to taste her Southern Comfort. Not from her glass.

Hitting the Bottle

The Dellen brothers, twins, lived at the corner of a typical Midwestern subdivision and while the 1960's churned out vast tracts of split level houses, the Dellens lived on the edge of the boom. They were on the outside looking in and lived a life apart from the suburban steel mill workers and business people inside the tract. Their small cottage was a holdout at the entrance to the post-war boom. They grew their own food. They were all heavy-set because they ate starch and low country food at a constant rate. The Dellen garden was over two acres, which amounted to eight subdivision houses worth of land.

That summer, the boys, Stewart and Malcolm swore they would defeat the game. The premise was simple enough: The carnival agent had a board about a foot square sitting on the counter of a four-square booth in the middle of the midway. He would lay a large Coke bottle on the board and challenge the mark to upright the bottle with the side of a finger. "Just lift up the bottle, boy and get it to sit upright!" For years, the Dellen boys would fight this battle of simple physics. The bottle would almost always teeter at the last second and fall over. Your money was gone and the big stuffed animal still sat upon the carny's shelf. So this year, Stewart and Malcolm, the double Dellens constructed an exact model of the carnival game. *The Bottle Tip*. They practiced the game with an intensity little known to their age group. Day and night, the bottle would be raised gingerly by the neck and flop over in the opposite direction. How could such a stupid thing be so hard to do? Practice yielded a small percentage of successful results. The boys continued fund raising through their paper routes. The 4 cents per paper earned from delivering the Chicago Tribune and Sun Times would fuel the quest. One of them was going to win the bottle game. The carny would lose.

So the fair was within sight. The early August heat was melting most of Indiana in preparation for the Lake County Fair. Sure, the whole Dellen family would go and take in the sideshow and some rides. They would breeze through the agricultural stuff, because they had to justify, like everyone else, entering the gaming area of the midway. The Bottle Tip Game loomed.

They needed tickets. The ticket booth was at most three feet square with a door on the side and a window through which the transactions were made. The window and a little ledge for counting out change were set a little high so that you couldn't *quite* see the surface when change was counted. Little known to the Dellen boys, there was a reason for this. Sometimes the ticket sales person would make a *mistake* with the change and it would be very unlikely that the ticket buyer would notice. It was very hard to see the money being counted out and the ticket seller would exert pressure to move along. If you handed them a twenty-dollar bill, the ticket agent *could* pause just long enough for an excited buyer to leave some of the change on that high counter. It's called the *natural drop* in carny parlance and can *earn* an unscrupulous ticket seller a few hundred bucks extra each day of the fair. Exact change for ticket purchase was always a good idea, because getting nicked out of five bucks is the equivalent of delivering 125 newspapers and walking several miles in the rain.

So, with tickets in hand the rides could commence. It would be a challenge to see who could withstand the Rock-O-Plane the most trips and live to tell about it. The sheer terror of climbing on the contraption and then feeling the G-force increase as it cranked up was worth the price. The Bottle Tip Game would wait for a little while and the guts could be churned up a bit. Add a few corn dogs, some cotton candy to the mix and you had a volatile and potentially explosive vessel. Danger lurked both inside and out.

A few hours into the evening, the draw of the midway joints became too strong and the allotted money for rides ran out. It was time for some serious gambling and the boys headed to the Bottle Tip. The carny running the game looked familiar. Maybe the same guy that took their money every year. This year was gonna be different. Stewart Dellen had practiced the game just as much as Malcolm, but didn't have the Lucky Mojo going for him. Stu played a few warm-up attempts and got close once or twice, but it was Malcolm with the magic. The empty sixteen-ouncer from the Coca-Cola Company rose slowly, barely pressing on Malcolm's bent index finger. The travel was only a few inches, but it took *eons*. The bottle was psychically willed to stand upright. On this day Malcolm Dellen became a winner. The bottle rocked a little and then stuck in the middle of the platform. Neat trick. The other boys at the fair from the subdivision behind the Dellen's couldn't have done it. They didn't do it. This game was rigged so tight that no one was supposed to win. But Malcolm loaded up his prize, his newly found pride and moved on. He moved on to the service, and made a career of it. He probably didn't see it as a turning point in his life, but it was. It was one of those small victories that change a day and one of those days that change a month. Everyone knows that a good month is all it takes to pick you up and embolden you past a lousy test score or a fuzzy future.

Frog & Harry

"If you can keep your head when all about you are losing theirs….." Not a possible situation for Frog, a Steele's Amusements ride boy. Frog and his friend liked to push the envelope; Racing trains. The idea, however stupid, is to race alongside a speeding train, overcome it and cross in front at a RR crossing; and live. The point scoring is binary. Win or lose. Live or die. Frog lost the last round one night in Wheeler, Indiana. The Porter County Sheriff's deputy lifted Frog's severed head from the ground and gingerly placed it into the trunk of his patrol car. A final act of dredging the shallow end of the gene pool.

Frog, actually Robert Boyer, was the quintessential ride boy. O.K., posthumously awarded the honorary title of ride jock, he lived in a cardboard box in back of the Rock-O-Plane. His life was not all that tragic, after all, it was a very nice cardboard box, a Frigidaire, or maybe the box the big Teddy Bears came in. Frog and his buddy, Tom Dunn, had picked up the hobby of train racing for lack of other summer excitement. It was a sad commentary on the risks of youth.

Harry the Artist

In order for the show to go on, the trucks and rides had to be painted. Not just any paint job would do. This is Show Business. The lettering on the trucks, rides and ticket booths had to be, well, showy.

"Hello, Steele's Amusements." Buck was manning the phones and snagged the call from out in Winter Quarters' massive barn-like structure. It was cold and the heat, well, the building had no heat. If you wanted paint to dry or plumbing to work, you had to go into the restroom with the salamander heater. No frills. What was that crap about 'in like a lion out like a lamb?' Bullshit. In Indiana March is always torture all month long.

"Hey Buck!" A woozy sounding guy was hailing Al (Buck) Steele from somewhere far away. At least it sounded far away because the call was coming from a phone booth at a truck stop. The telephone operator broke in: "Will you accept a collect, person-to-person call from a Harry Crumms?" Obviously the operator was having some trouble understanding the language of liquor. Buck immediately recognized the voice of Harry Crippins and paused to reflect for a moment. He had been expecting this call from Harry, and he did need the sign work done. Some of the rides were being re-themed and Harry was the guy to do it. This was always a test of wills and patience. Harry Crippins was the carnival artist for Steele's Amusements and an uncommon talent. Buck had to start early in the year to bring Harry from his home base in Florida to Valparaiso, Indiana. Crippins always started the process by requesting a $50 retainer to begin his trip.

"Like I have any choice?" Buck exhaled to the operator. "Sure, put him on. Harry, where the Hell are you?"

"I think I'm just outta' Gainesville or so." Harry burped into the telephone. Pity the next guy to use that phone booth, Buck thought.

"Let me guess, you need a few dollars to buy, say, bus-fare to get to Valpo?" "That's about the size of it podna." Crippins slurred into the phone.

"OK, how about I send you fifty bucks for transport and you hump it up here damn quick." Al always started to exert some urgency into the negotiation at this point to break through the alcohol haze. "Where can I send the dough to, Harry?"

"Well, let me see..." There was a long pause as Harry, no doubt, was looking for some written sign of where he was on Earth. "Uh, Buck?"

"Yeah, Harry."

"I'm at the Mobil Truck Service Area in, er, Tallahassee."

"Harry, Tallahassee is pretty far from Gainesville. You sure you know where you are?"

"Oh, uh, yeah. I got a ride from this guy from Gainesville and he brung me to this... Mobil stop. It was pretty late and I forgot..."

"Never mind, Harry. I'll get the money to you. Just make sure you catch a ride up here right away. We're not getting any younger." Buck was mentally calculating the distance from Florida, not in miles, but in bottles and cans. He could expect Harry Crippins in about three weeks.

Somewhere around Valdosta, Georgia, Harry contacted Buck again for another $50. Valdosta was only sixty miles or so from his last call, but prices for booze must have been working against him. Sometime later, Harry checked in again from

Memphis, Tennessee and asked for a final $50 for some minor, imagined emergency. It took about a month, but Crippins eventually showed up in Indiana. Harry then listed for Buck what art supplies and paints he needed. Harry traveled light and didn't burden himself with trade tools. Buck needed to get these supplies as fast as he could before Harry decided to leave again. Harry was a nomad.

Buck wrote out the art supply list he needed for Harry and planned to drive to his supplier in Gary, Indiana to fill the order.

No one in their right mind wanted to drive to 16th and Broadway in Gary to buy anything. Gary, Indiana always vied for title as Murder Capitol of the U.S.A., and that area of midtown was the epicenter. Still, they had a small paint factory that produced a highly pigmented paint so that truck lettering could be done in one coat cutting the labor and time needed in half. It was called One-Shot and Buck figured that was all he had; *one shot* at getting this work done. Since Harry couldn't be trusted to stick around for two coats of paint, this risk and expense was worth it. Buck hopped into the Ford and headed West along U.S. 30.

Instead of circumventing the dangerous ghetto area of Gary's East side, Buck took, as usual, the scenic route straight through town. (In the 1970's the term 'ghetto' was still in use, only because a more derogatory one could not be found.) The North-South corridor of Broadway connected suburban, predominantly white Merrillville with the violent Steel City of Gary, Indiana. Buck drove with purpose and, as was proper, caution. Crossing the bridge over the I-94 expressway was like interplanetary travel. Suddenly the relative wealth of one town disappeared into the squalor of another. The locals used to jokingly call Gary, Indiana 'Plywood Minnesota' because most of the storefronts along its central street were boarded up. The other joke they said was, "last one out of Gary, turn out the lights.' On the street Buck could see the beginnings of a fashion trend. Men with wide-brimmed hats and faux seal fur coats strutted along Broadway during working hours. Stores like Tom Olesker's specialized in *The Pimp Chic* look. It was created in these neighborhoods and exported all over.

The paint store, Consumers Paint was a retail outlet for the factory further downtown. Buck hoped to be able to fill the order with paint from the store shelf and spare himself another hour in decaying urban Hell. Parking next to an abandoned Caddy DeVille, he dashed into the small storefront. Why is it, he thought, that these old shopkeepers are so fearless? The counter guy, an old Jewish man had to be about 80 years old and seemed perfectly OK with working in this area. We need these tough old buzzards in Vietnam, not here, Buck thought. The store had the stuff, even the standard cream and orange; Steele's Amusements signature colors. Buck was in business as long as he could get Harry on task.

Retracing his route past some guys dressed like John Shaft, Buck decided running all the red lights would be appropriate. It was getting late. This was less of a place to be after dark than before. Time was of the essence. The relative safety of Valparaiso beckoned.

"Harry, I think you should start with the Dark Ride. We're gonna change it to 'Haunted Diggin's, you know, kind of a Halloween, graveyard type theme."

"It's your dime, Buck, but we usually close up before Halloween. Don't 'ya think people will see the, um, the flaw?"

"It's a goddam carnival ride, Harry! People don't see anything but your paint job. After they get in, it's dark anyway. Please, just paint the thing."

"Buck, you want me to paint *the THING* too? Harry obviously referring to the carnival ride named, The THING.

"My head is killing me. Look, paint the first thing that we discussed and then, come to think of it, paint that *Thing* you mentioned too. Just don't leave town before you finish every-

THING."

Through Harry's alcoholic mental maze, he made a point that the THING attraction could use some paint as well.

You might think that having the DT's would be a disadvantage in the hand lettering and art business, but Harry was a master of compensation. He used a bar and ball tool to steady his hand, which might be shaking like mad on its own, but would steady right up when he leaned into the lettering bar.

The important thing about carnival graphics was their lack of subtlety. They weren't designed for art appreciation class; they are intended to catch the eye of hyperactive kids and adults. There's a lot of stuff at a carnival to grab your attention, but the rides have to compete to make money. Harry did display a high level of skill in his work, but kept it simple enough to be effective.

The sideshow graphics and banners tended to be more elaborate than the rides. There was a reason for this. With a ride, what you see is what you get and the graphics are only part of the draw to the thing. After all, you can see the actual ride machinery behind the sign and you know what is in store. This isn't the case with parts of the midway sideshow. With, particularly, the Pickled Punk parts of the sideshow, the banners and art are really the whole show. It is almost a guarantee that seeing premature, deformed babies floating in formaldehyde will disappoint you. A jar with a punk is the same almost everywhere. The whole draw has to be at the entrance with flashy graphics. Crippins was good at developing great expectations only to be dashed by reality. No better example of this was the sign that hawked 'Little Dora Willard, the Cyclops Girl." The canvas banner showed a smiling, joyful youngster in a blue dress riding a bicycle. She had ONE BIG EYE in the middle of her forehead; great picture, great carnival painting. The customer plunked down some money and went into the trailer expecting to see something ALIVE and spectacular. Well, Little Dora Willard just sat there in a gallon jar all shriveled up. She actually does only have one eye. This attraction doesn't rely on repeat business, but the artwork brought in new suckers season after season. It also brought back a few sickos and those with diminished memory.

Harry Crippins had but a short time to finish the painting. Soon, either the Steele's would have to hit the road or his own demons would scare him off. Harry was a nomad, but he was an important cog in the carnival operation. When Harry Crippins was done, the "Show Beautiful" was ready to play.

Licensed to Kill

Long and dull, Highway 12 from Elkhorn, Wisconsin to Lancaster is a simple stretch. It stands as the final leg on a carnival journey from Nowhere, USA to the safe haven of Winter Quarters, Valparaiso, Indiana. It's the end of the season and this has been a long, mind-numbing march. The year, 1976 had been as rough as they come. Buck and the crew were ready for one last blast before parking Steele's Amusements for good. Finish Elkhorn and make for the border. Finish Elkhorn and get 24 trucks, various felons, and a load of cash from the land of cheddar through Illinois, to Valparaiso. But the lawman stands in the way. Driving through the night, one of the lead truck drivers notices that he is out of matches. It was imperative that he should pull the rig over and flag down another truck, hopefully driven by another degenerate smoker. As both semis sat on the roadside, a Wisconsin State Trooper pulled over to check out the scene. These boys could need assistance, and that's what the Wisconsin State Police are there for; to serve and protect.

This being a routine check, Barney Fife decides to examine the first carny's driver's license. Arkansas driver's license and Indiana truck plates. It's been known to happen. Copper looks at the other carny's license and registration; same Arkansas D.L., same expiration date. Copper tempted to let them both go, but starts thinking....Lot of Arkansas guys in Wisconsin on this particular evening. Trooper Prentiss, his real name, has a Eureka! moment. The driver's licenses were filled in with ink, hand written dates and names. Copper sets up a roadblock and starts pulling in every semi from the highway.

Buck thought that it would be a good idea, some time ago, to order a 12-pack of driver's licenses from an Arkansas guy he knew. Most of his guys had no driver's license. It was a simple expedient to write to his Arkansas buddy and buy a stack in bulk. It saves time. It saves money. They were real enough for most purposes. Buck retained his own Indiana license even if he forgot to renew it from time to time. Some numbskull had filled all the licenses in with the same information, with an ink pen?

Buck's was the last semi to be pulled over. He would have been home free except for two things: His legit driver's license was expired and he was in charge of all the other miscreants. The trooper insisted that he do the responsible thing and come into the station with the whole lot.

The cops decided that all twelve carnies should go to the sheriff's office to figure this out; lined up on a bench; Buck and the crew.

By now Buck had spent a good part of the evening with Trooper Prentiss. The fool was squandering his authority. Was he looking for a payoff? The officious cheddar-head was really milking this period of phony indecision. Where was this going? Didn't he hear the legal argument laid out before him? The odds of stopping twelve consecutive vehicles each with a driver's license expiring on June 11 is, of course, unusual. But the odds are finite. There is a mathematical explanation to this phenomenon. What does it matter how long the odds are? Coincidences happen all the time! So what if all the drivers were from Arkansas? There are at least five million residents from that poor southern state. They all have to be somewhere at any given time. Some are in Wisconsin at roughly the same time. "What do you mean you're impounding the trucks?" This logical train of discussion was going nowhere but to the poky. A shift in strategy would be needed fast. The copper was closing his mind to perfectly good, if novel, explanations of events. "So, officer, of course we will cooperate in every way. After all we are honest business people. Entertainers, in fact, on our way to cheer up throngs of kids; actually, sick kids. That's right, we're going to see very sick kids unable to get in on the Ronald Donald thing or whatever. But heck, we are good Americans after all. Sure, we'll go along with this error, or snafu, you know, as a matter of good relations with the police. Did you notice that F.O.P. sticker on my rear window? Yes, we dump a load of money on the F.O.P. each year. Of course, we're not looking for any special favors, no; we just want to show our colors, so to speak. So, officer, has your station received it's stack of complimentary carnival tickets as yet? No? Let's just step over to the business trailer for a moment and correct that oversight before we finish business here." The copper was taking the bait in a cautious manner. Reel him in. "Now since you have so correctly called in backup units, I'd say enough to quell a small riot, we had better go with you to the station to make this all look on the up and up. I certainly wouldn't squawk about a small fine to justify your efforts, either. Come to think of it, you could have a promotion on the way and could use some good paper to cinch that."

They rolled to the county lockup. The situation seemed to be tempering a little. Deputy Dog was relaxing and his demands for a full investigation and exorbitant bail were finally losing steam. The look of all the boys lined up on a hard bench, handcuffed like a bunch of scum was disheartening. What kind of railroad job was this? These guys couldn't just get driver's licenses any old time they wanted. We had a show to put on. Besides, they all had special needs and problems. Not all of them were fighting totally irresponsible DUI charges in other states. Some of these guys had legitimate learning disabilities that made them bad test takers. That's right! These charges were in fact a form of illegal discrimination. What kind of Gestapo outfit would deprive an educationally handicapped man from making a decent living? We all know Wisconsin could be some kind of Hell, but this was the proverbial straw.

"Sure officer, your men can drive all the trucks to the county jail. Please tell them to be extraordinarily careful though. You see, we have, for instance, many rare biological specimens floating in jars of corrosive, very noxious, preservative. This unique display is irreplaceable and must be protected at all costs. Should one of your able, but unpracticed officers jolt these specimens, or cause a load shift, we cannot be held responsible for the potential hazard resulting. I can see a lengthy lane closure, chemical burns, yes, and a danger to the general populace if an accident should happen. By the way, do you have a specific area-wide evacuation plan? Just curious. Well, let's move this on. We only have a few hours to settle this and get set up for the Sick Children's Carnival."

Buck and the trooper climbed into the Ford police cruiser and pulled out onto the highway, gaining speed. The trucks, all by now piloted by nervous sheriff's deputies slowly ground gears and crawled back onto the pavement. The convoy of police cars and trucks flowed like viscous liquid to the HQ. Chat in the lead car between Buck and Trooper Prentiss was genial. "Kids? Sure, we both have 'em, don't we? Little buggers really keep you guessing. Have to set an example every waking minute. You notice no animus here. Important for the youngsters to know how to respect authority. You'll notice kids with the carnival are a very respectful, obedient bunch. Brought up on hard work and an appreciation for a buck." "By the way," Buck sticks his hand toward the trooper, "my friends call me Buck!" The trooper was forced to shake hands while driving down the highway.

When the long caravan of carnival trucks came to a stop at the Grant County Jail, one deputy crawled out from behind the wheel and approached Buck with a distraught look. "Look, pal..." the deputy said, "You give those guys hazard pay for driving these wrecks?" Buck explained all too fully, "I knew you boys might have some trouble with these rigs. Some of them have a vacuum line problem that makes going up and down hills a little dicey. It takes some time to get used to. Glad everyone made it back without incident."

The fine was nominal. Maybe it made it to the county coffers, maybe not.

Cost: $180.00, still in the positive column by most accounting methods. To top it off, Trooper Prentiss got some part-time work helping Buck put up the giant Steele's Amusements Ferris Wheel. Upon leaving, the trooper carefully informed the crew of Steele's Amusements of his patrol schedule. It would be good, he explained if they all left Wisconsin for home before he had to patrol that area again. There is a moral to this story, but not one to give to the kids. Breaking the law is one thing, but treating the lawmen with some respect can change the direction of conflict.

Carny versus the Mob

Something is missing here. A piece left out. We can see how L.E. Steele got from the Depression to the carnival business and how he brought his kids and grandkids into the show. But there was another factor, a compelling one that caused the Steele's to go through the carnival door and never turn back. The Mob.

In the late '50's the Steele family did some carnival work during the summer and various other jobs in the winter. They hadn't yet bought the full complement of rides and equipment from Snapp's and they hadn't yet made the commitment to 'go for broke'. Al Steele Sr. had one foot in the carnival business and one foot out. The foot that was 'out' was busy using his summertime arcade equipment, like pinball machines and games to supplement their income. Each fall, Al Sr. would take the pinball machines out of the penny arcade trailer and place them in local businesses. He would travel around to bowling alleys, fraternity houses and truck stops collecting coins from the machines and splitting these proceeds with the 'hosting' business. After servicing the games he would be on his way. As this business grew, Al found that he could rent more machines from a Chicago manufacturer and expand into more areas. Town by town and eventually into neighboring counties, Al Steele made another business for himself. This did not go unnoticed by the Chicago boys.

Al had crossed an invisible line. He had purchased a number of 8-Ball machines that were commonly used by taverns as moneymaking entertainment. The difference between one of these machines and a regular pinball machine was that the player could pump in larger amounts of money and play greater odds of winning. The payoffs could be large, reflected in a high point score. If a player won, the bartender would fork over winnings based on the score racked on the machine. These were used as gambling machines in the days before video poker. Gambling was the sole province of a certain group of organized business people in the area and these people were not happy with Al Steele Sr.

" 'Ya know, Al, the worst thing you can do is take away another persons livelihood." The man was jabbing a short, sausage-like finger into Al's chest. Al had gone to a service call in LaPorte, Indiana to see one of his pinball machines. Person or persons unknown had pounded one machine into dust with a sledgehammer. This man with oregano on his breath was now explaining some things to Al. The man was flirting with a fractured skull. No Steele and especially Al Steele ever allowed this type of confrontation without immediate response, but for once, Al kept his fists at bay.

"I'm not following you. First off, who are you?" Al was real irritated. There was this bystander or witness to the incident inches in front of him giving something like a speech right into his face.

"It's not so important who I am as who I speak for. You gotta problem here."

"I'll say I have a problem here. I have an expensive piece of equipment turned to shit. Someone has to pay for this. You do this? I ought'a sledgehammer you!"

"Yeah, well before you pull out the tools and hardware you better listen careful. Our friends," Al gulped as he heard the famous Mafia code term, "Our friends are tired of this shit. You moving into this county with your machines is fucking up our business interests. We're tired of it and you gotta go. Go back to Porter County where you belong. Pull these things out of here and life will go on as per usual. Leave 'em here and you're gonna get hurt." The little fat man was not interested in a two-way conversation.

"I'll see about that..." Steele said calmly.

"Yeah, problem is, the next time we talk about this, you won't see nothin'." The little man turned and walked down the sidewalk without conviction. He wasn't going away, Al thought. He was told to stick around and watch. Make sure those 8-Ball machines disappeared.

Al Steele Sr. was a pragmatist. The expansion into LaPorte County with his pinball business was not profitable enough to fight the Mob over. He had a family to think of. These people were not the types you can reason with.

The machines came out of LaPorte and were relocated to

Lake County, Indiana. This may not have been a good move, since even from the Capone days, Lake County was a Mob suburb of Mob Chicago. LaPorte was a backwater compared to Lake County and it's main cesspool, Gary, Indiana. Al Steele was flying dangerously close to the flame.

The next contact was predictable in its subject but unpredictable in its delivery. Al got a call from someone claiming to be from the Lake County, Indiana Prosecutor's office. It seems that they would like to talk to him about his business in Lake County. The alleged prosecutor's man, George was concerned that Al had placed some pinball machines at a truck stop just over the county line. George was not concerned about the legal status of the machines but more about whose territory they were encroaching upon. George made it clear that there was an arrangement in Lake County about the placement of gambling equipment and Al was not now, nor ever would be part of that arrangement. The machines had to go.

Still smarting from the LaPorte encounter, Al was reluctant to take this demand at face value. The machines stayed at the truck stop.

George called again and wanted to meet with Al. "Steele,

why don't we take a ride and chat about this. I'll be right over to pick you up."

"I can't make it today, but tomorrow I'm gonna be around here. Let me tell you where I live. You take Route 30..." Al was cut off.

"Yeah, I know where you live." George said sarcastically. "I'll come around tomorrow morning and we'll talk about things in my car." Al deflected the attempt to meet at his home in Valparaiso. Better to meet someplace very public.

Al, Sr. needed to think fast and prepare for this. The man was adamant that they would have to take a ride to discuss things. That didn't sound good. Al called over to his son, Al Jr. or Buck, the law school student and his brother Vinnie. He explained the situation and they devised a plan. Both would come to the Lake County restaurant meeting place in a Ford pickup truck. They would be dressed like a couple of grease monkeys in coveralls and packing .38 caliber police specials. Al's backup team was in place and would be staking out the restaurant parking lot during the meeting, then Buck and Vinnie would hang a loose tail on Al and the mobster to make sure things didn't get out of hand.

The next day the supposed Lake County Prosecutor's man came barreling down the highway and pulled into the restaurant parking lot. "C'mon Steele, let's go sightseeing." George motioned to the passenger door as he popped the lock.

The ride out of southern Lake County started out quiet. George seemed friendly enough, if not a little rough around the edges. He seemed a lot like a county cop or investigator in plain clothes but didn't want to talk about his county position.

"This is beautiful country. I love the quiet secluded areas out here." George started to wax poetic and Al wondered why he stupidly agreed to take this ride in the country. One good thing: George didn't notice Vinnie and Buck trailing them about a quarter of a mile back. If he did, he didn't say anything about it. Al thought about this being something Buck wouldn't learn in law school.

"You know, Al I think we should go up North. I like the countryside and all, but I am a city boy at heart. Why don't we head toward, say, Hammond?"

"Not being a city boy, I don't really care to see Hammond or even E. Chicago for that matter. Why don't you cut to the chase and tell me what you want from me?" Al was getting nervous. This ride was looking like one of those last rides the Mob is so famous for.

"I'm really enjoying myself here, why make this all business? I say we go up North and maybe catch a sandwich or something. Great day for a ride." George was grinning, with his eyes glued onto Route 41 and heading north. They had already passed the jail that had held Dillinger and Al Capone's old stomping grounds in the south county. The Chicago Outfit boys loved this area. They had control and very little to worry about. They owned Lake County.

After making the rounds up north, George turned back towards Crown Point and the county courthouse. Now the explanation came. "You see, Al, I could'a killed you anywhere from the boondocks down south to the city in North Hammond. Anywhere. Nobody would have seen anything and nobody would have cared. You might remember this guy up in Kenosha a few months ago? He was foolin' in things he had no business to. That guy was interferin' in our friends business by puttin' machines in taverns there.

"That guy is now dead. He is buried in that black Wisconsin soil. You get the point I'm makin' here?" George coasted to a stop in front of the Lake County Courthouse. "Now get the fuck out and go home and I don't care how you get there. Do not come back to Lake County for anything." Just as George finished, a Ford pickup truck kissed his back bumper, and Al spoke.

"You might have been able to kill me anywhere you want. On the other hand, my brother and my son, right in back of us here," Al nodded toward the truck now touching the back bumper, "would have killed you next. You know where I live, but I know where you work. You stay out of my way and I'll stay out of yours, and that includes Lake County, Indiana. This is ended for now." Al got out of George's car and rode with his family back to Porter County. He wished that this ended things, but he knew in his gut that it didn't.

Throughout the following months, Al Sr. minded his own business, staying in Valparaiso and tending to pinball machines and 8-Ball machines in Porter County only. He was determined not to take that next ride offer by the Outfit man from Lake County.

Buck Steele continued in law school. He was a second year law student at Valparaiso University and helped his father from time to time in the business. Al, Sr. owned a pool hall called 'The Billie Club'. It had a semi-permanent card game going and also operated a few 8-Ball machines in an upstairs room over the pool tables. Once, Al asked Buck to go and remove one of the older 8-Balls. The machine had been malfunctioning and needed to be replaced. Buck arrived at the club and ran into his Valparaiso Law School contracts professor. The professor was a card game regular and seemed to have a passing familiarity with the gambling machines as well. Feeling good that his father's pool hall at least had law school sanction, Buck continued his work. In those days there was gambling and then there was Gambling. Nobody seemed to be bothered by the friendly game of stud poker; or a pinball machine; well, almost nobody.

Buck's legal education moved along two tracks, one in an accredited law school and one on the streets of Middle America. Each week, when a county official came by, it was Buck's job to place bottles of whiskey and a bag of cash in the back of his car. The political shakedown was a fixture of the Porter County establishment and Buck learned that right along with torts in school.

The local county officials were conflicted. Some of the townspeople wanted to rid Valparaiso of these gambling machines. It was an election year. Mayor Wiggins bowed to pressure and sent city police to confiscate the 8-Balls from The Billie Club. Everyone wanted Al out of the pinball business; the Mob and the politicians. Al's response to the Chief of Police went something like this:

"You know damn well where they are, you were playing them just last week." Al Sr. was responding to what seemed like a really dumb question. The Chief wanted to know where his contraband gambling machines were. Guess he had to play the roll.

"Al, we have to take them 8-Balls out and lock 'em up, so don't give us any trouble." The Chief was apologetic.

"No trouble from me. On the other hand, you ever hear about the Fourth Amendment? The part of the Constitution that refers to a warrant?"

"We don't have no arrest warrant Al, we just need to get the machines!" The Chief was getting a little agitated.

"No, I was more thinking of a search warrant. The Constitution does have something to say about search and seizure..." Al trailed off when decided that his beef was with the Mayor, not his good friend the police chief. The Mayor had clearly put the cops on the spot by insisting on the equipment seizure. Wiggins wanted to mollify the restless natives during an election year. He was not about to let a small thing like the U.S. Constitution get in the way.

"Yeah, well you settle up those little details with the Mayor, Al, we gotta git these things outta' here." The cops would find out soon enough that the machines were heavy and not easy to move. Al wondered which ones would try to take them out of the second story places and carry them down the narrow stairways. The local cops weren't that energetic anyway.

After a time, Al Sr. threatened to sue the City of Valparaiso and the Mayor over illegal seizure of his pinball machines. The Mayor knew he didn't have a legal leg to stand on and returned the machines to Steele. Al placed the machines in other towns throughout the county, mostly further south, out of the easy reach of the corrupt northern Porter County Democratic machine.

Late in 1958, the war on organized crime was heating up and the Kennedy brothers, Jack and Bobby were using their anticrime activities for a springboard to the White House. Bobby Kennedy was chief counsel for the U.S. Senate rackets committee and sent one of his senior staffers to investigate organized crime in Northwest Indiana. Richard Sinclair, Bobby's point man and investigator contacted the Porter County Sheriff's Police deputy chief, Harold Rayder. Kennedy wanted to investigate the Mob's ties to the vending business in Lake and Porter counties. Chief Rayder knew whom to call. He had heard of the unpleasant contacts Al Steele had with certain elements of his business and knew Al would be a trove of information.

Sinclair, Rayder and Steele began to meet at regular intervals to plot strategy, but it was the Chicago Mob that made contact first. Gaetano "Tommy" Morgano reputed Outfit boss for Northwest Indiana called on Chief Rayder. He wanted to make some kind of accommodation so that his boys could own the Porter County pinball business. He wanted official sanction to get Al Steele out of the business. He wanted to have a confidential talk with Rayder to iron out the details.

Morgano owned a pizza joint in Valparaiso, near the university. It was common for the Outfit to operate from pizza parlors, but this one was far afield from more visible operations in Lake County. Morgano's operations in Porter County flew well under the radar. There were several rumors about when and where Morgano first made contact with the Porter County Chief Deputy. Everyone agrees that Morgano made the first move in proposing a meeting and stepped right into a trap. It was the crime boss's turn to take a ride with Steele's.

Under Bobby Kennedy's direction, Sinclair wired Rayder to record the meeting. Tommy Morgano had guessed wrong when he thought that this particular cop was for sale. Tommy picked up Chief Rayder and drove around Valparaiso looking for a place to talk. Whether just standard operating procedure or from a justified suspicion, Morgano acted to foil any attempt at recording. He pulled into a noisy factory parking lot. Any recording device would have trouble picking up the low tones of conversation from the industrial sounds of McGill's Bearing factory. In the parking lot, Morgano explained to the Chief that he would provide $50,000 if Rayder would get Steele out of the way and turn a blind eye to whatever Tommy wanted to do. Later, the tape was played. The sound quality was poor, the background noisy, but good enough that Bobby Kennedy could advance his investigation. Kennedy told Sinclair to set up a meeting with Al Steele.

On a cold wet March 1959 evening, Bobby Kennedy rolled into Valparaiso, Indiana. Led by Sinclair, they went to meet Al Steele at his home on Route 30. The freezing rain soaked Bobby that night and, as he stood inside Steele's front door, he asked Al's wife Maytha if he could remove his wet shoes and socks. After politely gaining permission, he sat barefooted in front of the fireplace, feet warming and discussing the Senate testimony process. Al Steele would be needed in Washington to testify before the U.S. Senate's racketeering subcommittee.

In June 1959, Al and Buck boarded a Lockheed Electra and made it to Washington. Al was ushered into the witness waiting room and as luck would have it had to sit next to Tommy Morgano. It was an awkward moment as the mobster confronted Al about his pending testimony. Morgano told Al calmly. "'Ya know Steele, you and I both came up the hard way. We respect you. So, no matter what you say today nothin' is gonna happen to you or your family. I don't work that way. But when this is all over and we are back in Indiana, I want to talk to you about buying you out of the pinball business. Straight business deal. No bullshit." Al sensed that the Outfit man was serious. An attempt to sway his testimony? Maybe, but is was too late to change anything now.

Buck had made his way into the audience seating well before his father's testimony. Sitting next to a former Porter County Sheriff, Buck noticed that most of the audience was in the Mob uniform of the day. Silk suits.

The former county sheriff leaned over and whispered. "Bucky, no money ever changed hands, right?" The cop wanted an answer now.

"No." Buck knew that nothing in law school had prepared him for this. His dad testifying to congress had made a lot of people nervous. The Mob had a good reason to be concerned, but so did the crooked politicians and cops that helped the Outfit flourish in Indiana. Morgano was a big fish, and the Steeles were messing up the pond. Buck had to watch what he said and watch his back.

Steele's testimony was well planned and Kennedy used it to make his case against Morgano. The gambling conviction and deportation of the Mob boss would mark a turning point in the Chicago Outfit's history. Their hold on Northwest Indiana was loosened.

Al Steele met with Tommy Morgano back in Valparaiso, just as Tommy had suggested. Morgano didn't seem to hold a grudge.

"OK, we know how many machines you have out and we know where they are. Anybody can rent machines. The real issue here is competition. It doesn't make sense to beat our brains out over this county, so, Al, what will it take to buy your business? I'm being reasonable here, and I expect you to be the same." Tommy was surprisingly calm considering the charges hanging over his head.

"Tommy, I wanna go into the carnival business full-time. I have the rides and equipment part figured out, but I need cash to build a Winter Quarters on Route 30 to house the trucks and equipment in the off-season. I need $17,000 for the building and would sell my pinball business for that. If you can do that, I will be out of your hair." Al Sr. had made a reasoned proposal. After a number of death threats, testifying against the Mob and worrying about his kids, he decided to get away from these people as cleanly as possible. The price was low. Tommy was astonished. If he would have gone this route in the first place, he might not be in the trouble he was in. Just bribing the cops in Porter County would have cost him much more than buying the competition out; a lesson learned much too late.

The deal was sealed and Al Sr. got his money. Plans were made to construct Winter Quarters in Valparaiso. The carnival was ready to go on the road, and Al Steele was one of the few to tangle with the Mob and walk away without a scratch. There were some tense times as Al and his family contemplated the possibility that he might have to do some prison time. They all wondered whether the feds were going after the really bad guys or looking to rip out the pinball business, roots and all. In retrospect it's obvious that the government's case and interests fell to the splashy, politically profitable campaign against the Mob. The Chicago Outfit was very close to the Democrat hierarchy in Chicago and was afforded some protection. After all, the 1960 presidential race was just ahead, and the Kennedys needed the support of Mayor Daley and the well-oiled Chicago political apparatus. Northwest Indiana, just minutes away from Chicago, was a showy enough target to be worthwhile, but not so essential to the Outfit that they couldn't deal with some setbacks.

For his part, Al Steele was grateful to be alive and starting into his new business. He thought it was ironic that Snapp, the *honest* Missouri bank executive that he dealt with for rides and equipment did more to cheat the Steeles than the mobster Tommy Morgano did. Winter Quarters was built on schedule and Steele's Amusements went on the road.

Czarny

"Whee-ah-zuh, thee-ah-zuh, bee-ah-zeef?" Buck questioned the jointee in perfectly clear, clipped czarny, the secret trade language of carnies. In English, the question was: "What's the beef?" It seemed that a customer was playing a game at a booth and thought he should have won a big prize. A monster Teddy Bear. The jointee running the game disagreed. The player was cheating and he was caught. There was no way the jointee was going to pay up to a cheat. In comes the 'patch.' Buck was always the patch or the fixer. The final arbiter of customer complaints. In the carny world, unlike the legal arbitration business, most negotiations are carried out in the open with all parties present. This can be trouble unless you can talk confidentially using czarny, the carnival operators' secret language.

The jointee responded, "Thee-ah-zis, me-ah-zark, ee-ah-zis, dree-ah-zunk! This mark is drunk! And clearly he was. The player, in some boozy haze had leaned way over the line to make his pitch while the jointee wasn't looking. Except the jointee is always looking. The guy cheated. Buck examined the economics of the situation.

"Hee-ah-zow, me-ah-zuch, he-ah-zas, spee-ah-zent?" How much has he spent? Buck wanted to know. No sense in getting into a brawl with a guy this drunk over a few dollars. The jointee explained that the drunk had dropped ten dollars already on a three- dollar prize and still hadn't won. The man was still a loser and still frustrated so he stretched the rules a little. Buck decided to blow the problem away.

"Sir, take your prize, but move on out of here. This just isn't your night." Buck muttered so that the jointee could hear, "pee-ah-zig." Pig.

Buck indicated to the jointee, again in czarny, that he should come to the office trailer later and settle up for the Teddy Bear. Life was too short to let these little problems take up your time.

Czarny is one of those staples of carnival life that tend to become more useful over time. It's easy enough to learn so that the 'undereducated' carnival employees can pick it up. One of the keys is speed. Since the language deception is fairly simple, it had to be used sparingly and quickly so that the marks couldn't understand what was being said. The usually high level of background noise that a carnival generates aided this. Unless the mark knew what to listen for, the Tilt-A-Whirl would run interference and help disguise the czarny language being spoken.

The construction of czarny is simple. You take the initial letter of a word and pronounce it with a long 'e' sound added. Then insert the syllable, 'ah' and finish the word by inserting a 'z'. Pig becomes 'Pee-ah-zig.' Dog becomes 'Dee-ah-zog.' Cat becomes 'Kee-ah-zat.' And so on. The ruse probably has the same origins as 'Pig-Latin.' Remember 'oot-fray-oops-lay?' but this version is called 'Z-Latin' for obvious reasons. The 'Zee' throws 'em every time.

The Steele's used to talk in czarny about those adult topics you don't want your kids to hear. It didn't take long for the kids to pick up the code, though, and after that, the youngest Steele's became experts in czarny.

Stardust Hotel, Las Vegas

Buck and crew climbed off the jetway of a Boeing 707 onto the tarmac of McCarron Airport. They arrived in Sin City with protection. Al Sr., Uncle Ray and Buck brought their spouses and a load of cash. The wives were along to keep them from doing anything stupid and the cash came along for a one-way ride. The goal of this mission was to get the Wisconsin Fair Board reps wined, dined, and more, in order to nail down a continuing string of good carnival spots for the next year. Buck knew the rules of this game. Vegas was and is a very rigged town. Carnies understand this process well. Nothing happens without the proper grease, and Buck had dug up a pile of one-hundred dollar bills to apply liberally within the mob inspired town.

Destination number one was the Stardust Hotel. The Stardust was as early Las Vegas project of the Boyd family, carny folks from the East Coast. The carny connection made the Steeles feel comfortable, but the other rumored connections gave them cause for concern. This was Vegas and everyone knew who pulled the strings. Try to mind your own business and nobody gets hurt. Right?

The check-in went OK, if you don't count the fifty bucks Al, Sr. had to fork over for the clerk to find the reservation. Memory lapses and missing paperwork are endemic in this town. After getting their personal rooms set up, the Steele's Board of Directors headed toward the lobby with their advertising posters. It was always a scramble to get up your advertising in as many places as you could before either the hotel management bitched or your competition got there; and boy was there competition. All the big carnivals from across the country were at the Stardust for the same purpose: Corral some business and attend the OABA meeting. The Outdoor Amusement Business Association was then and is today a trade group of carnies looking out for their own. There were battles to be fought on the legal front and Buck Steele, carnival attorney, was ready to go.

In the poster area of the lobby, Buck and Ray quickly set out the advertising and established the Steele's Amusements beachhead. From the other end of the poster area, Buck could see Jack Klemz, the carnival association director steaming toward them.

"Hello, Mr. Director, how the Hell are 'ya?" Buck was glad to see a fellow OABA board member.

"Buck, we have a situation to figure out. A couple of goons from the Teamsters were sent over to see us and they had one of those propositions that you can't refuse."

"What's their problem? We don't even have Teamsters working for us in the Midwest. We're just a bunch of seasonal workers...." Buck was preaching to the choir, and Klemz quickly interrupted him.

"No, listen, they don't give a shit whether we have card carrying members or not. You remember what they did to Vivona's? How many trucks did they sabotage by slashing tires and ripping radiators? This time they put a price tag on protection." Jack Klemz was speaking in short bursts. He was out of breath already.

Buck sensed a bottom line coming. "OK, Jack, what's the price-tag for healthy tires and cooling systems these days?"

"This blows me away. They want "X" dollars per employee sent to them each month. They don't care how we do it or account for it. No discounts. Get the cash there, and they said cash, or else."

"So, Jack, how do they expect to keep the FBI out of this shake-down? I mean, they just can't run a straight protection scam on us and expect we're gonna take it lying down." Buck was playing this out in his mind.

"They want to say they are providing health insurance to our people as a union benefit in exchange for the 'dues.' They don't care about the names of our guys or any other stuff, they just want to say they are providing insurance."

"Pretty businesslike of them. Oh, I get it. They want to keep us healthy? Who are these mobsters?"

"Joey and Phil. Lotta names end in vowels with this group. I'm not sure how we're gonna handle it, but we need to talk to the others."

Buck didn't like the idea of messing with Teamsters in Las Vegas. They have too many business relationships in this town. "OK, Jack, I can do the math. This is serious crap and we can deal with it in an executive session at the casino bar. Wait. Maybe our hospitality suite would be better. God knows who the bartender reports to." Buck clapped the shaken Klemz on the back and resumed his convention prep.

The Steeles were here to entertain fair board members and had to keep distractions to a minimum. Certain members of the Wisconsin boards would hold out signing contracts until the Las Vegas meeting. This ensured better treatment from the carnival operators as they vied for county fair business.

After softening up the Janesville and Elkhorn, Wisconsin customers with drinks and carny stories, Buck loaded them into a cab for some real pressure selling. Dinner. It was important to make them think twice before switching carnival midway contracts. Buck accomplished this by concentrating attention on these two key players.

"Sir, it seems we may have a table for you in, um, forty

minutes?" The maitre d' grinned at Buck waiting for a response. Buck knew where this was headed. They could stand in the long line for an hour and get a crappy table or pay up now and keep his customers happy. Buck peeled off the first of his crisp hundreds and pressed it into the restaurateur's hand. No more words were needed. The maitre d' spread his arms gesturing for the group to follow him into the dining area. Buck figured this guy must knock down a few thousand extra per day. Nice job.

Dinner was good and the cheese-heads were thrilled to hear Buck had tickets for Dean Martin's show. It was gonna be a late night.

About 4:00AM, as Buck was returning half dead to his room, he heard screaming from a suite on the opposite end of the hall. "(Something like) Stop! For God's sake STOP!" Buck wondered if he should call a cop, but then he remembered that one of the fair board guys had asked him for a fifty-dollar donation earlier to finance the entertainment of a young lady. It seems one of their group was newly divorced and the boys decided to cheer him up. Midmorning the leader of the fair contingent explained that his divorced friend was OK, but had to scream at the girl to keep her from stripping his gears, so to speak.

This first full day of OABA meetings was going to tackle more than just the Teamsters problem. The Teamsters had been a thorn in the collective carnival side for years. A fellow carny in Detroit told Buck that before he could drive his popcorn truck into the fairgrounds, he had to jump out and let a Teamster drive through the gate. The Teamster got paid about a dollar a foot to pull this off. So much for the fight to improve conditions for America's workers. No, there was serious legislative stuff on the agenda.

Adam Clayton Powell, Jr., U.S. congressman, had sent a representative around to the carnival owners and restaurant people. The rep had a list of business types that would, if Powell got his legislation through, be designated non-exempt for minimum wage purposes. This could cost the carnival industry a bundle. The rep did, however offer a way around the problem. If the carnival operators forked over a $50,000 donation to Powell's, er, 'Fund' the legislation would just go away. It had to be a cash transaction and it had to be now.

The OABA decided to pay a lobbyist to fight the wage and hour law changes. On the surface, the association seemed to be organized and willing to play the Washington game by the rules. Adam Clayton Powell, Jr. may not have had the same rules in mind. The OABA sent reps to Chicago to finance the lobbying effort. With $1500 in hand, the lobbyist went back to Washington and the following legislation did indeed exempt carnival operations from the new wage and hour law provisions. Was that all it took? $1500? It sounds like a great lobbying success story. But Buck had seen the hit list with his own eyes. Congressman Powell had a collection list of businesses that would be affected by the new law and then sent out the collector. It wasn't the first time that two levels of lobbying worked over a piece of legislation. The one you see and the one you don't.

There was one round of schmoozing to go before the Steeles flew back to Chicago and drove on to Valparaiso. Most of the big issues were out of the way and some trade talk was next. There was an exhibition area affiliated with the Stardust loaded with booths and sales people devoted to the carnival industry. It was customary to bring either a down payment for a new piece of equipment or a continuing payment to help a company justify the booth expense. Steele's had just purchased a large ride and brought in the appropriate amount of cash to make the vendor feel better. As Buck prepared to end another interesting convention meeting, a gentleman came up and introduced himself as 'Carbone' or 'Cardone'.

"Hey, Buckie Steele! How 'ya doin'? Glad to see 'ya here in Las Vegas! Hey, your kids still go to that Hayes Leonard School in Val-pie-rays-oh? You know the one, right off Route 30? Just wondered." The thick-necked thug was sending a message. "Hey, your wife still shops at Wiseway supermarket, right? They knew where Buck lived and where his kids could be found. They also knew where his wife shopped. They wanted to remind him of the Teamsters deal just one more time before they all left town. The union boys never did pay a single insurance claim with their protection money. The intersection of politics, crime and business lies in a grey area. Sometimes survival depends on navigating through that intersection.

First National Carny Bank

Carnies hate banks. They're never open when you need them. They always ask too many questions. Better just bury your money in a can. The best can is a Folger's 3 lb., with paraffin caked all over the top and sides. This provides optimal moisture protection for your currency. Just a reminder: It is not a good idea to check a carny's back yard to see if they continue this money saving trick. Carnies all have guns.

    The last thing Buck did after getting dressed was to roll up $150 in one dollar bills and cram them in his pocket. The First National Carny Bank was now open. Buck strolled out onto the midway to start the day.

A combination wake-up service, den mother, and loan officer, Buck was responsible for getting the workforce into gear and on task each day. Get 'em up, give 'em some lunch money, and get 'em working.

"Hey, Slick, you gonna make it?" This was a rhetorical question. Slick always made it. It wasn't always pretty, but he got to work somehow. Buck asked the next and most predictable question. "How much 'ya need today?"

Slick, barely thinking said. "'bout seven bucks, Buck." The less that Slick opened his mouth at this time the better. He knew what had gone into it, and wasn't quite sure what might come out yet. He was pretty sick. However Slick was able to utter the top amount allowed for morning advance. Buck nodded and peeled off seven one-dollar bills and passed them to his hung-over ride foreman. Pulling a pencil off his ear, the boss marked the draw book next to Slick's name. Slick was now in negative financial territory and would probably get a 'zero check' on payday. Which is to say that he had borrowed so much money day to day from Buck that it amounted to more than his weekly check.

Slick liked working it this way, knowing that at the end of the season he could even things up with his bonus money. The carnies all got generous bonuses at the end of the tour with Steele's. Some of them were far enough in the hole by then that even their bonus didn't square things. Buck usually just zeroed the account and loaned them bus fare to get to a girlfriend's house for the winter.

Wednesday was payday and the crew would be given checks, momentarily, for the work they had done for the week and through the previous night. They actually only had the paycheck for a few seconds, just long enough to endorse. Some just signed with an 'X'. Since banks have a real problem cashing checks for a person with no identification, no bank account and no address, the Steele's always instantly cashed employee checks and handed them the cash.

Once, the U.S. Department of Labor decided to do an audit of Steele's Amusements and go over this paycheck process. The auditor looked askance at the way Steele's handled the paperwork. Actually, Steele's Amusements did things by the book. They dutifully collected all the information needed to file employer tax returns.

The audit conversation went something like:

Auditor: Mr. Steele, we have chosen your company for audit based on the observation that most of your employees have invalid Social Security Numbers.

Buck: Hold on a minute! How do you know these numbers are no good? Are you saying that we have incorrect information represented on our W-4 forms? As you know, this information is provided by the employee on hiring. Business being like it is, we sometimes hire in the middle of a rainstorm standing in mud. So you see, it might not be the best time to scrutinize each data point for accuracy. I'm actually surprised to see that we have information on some of these guys at all. In fact, (Buck pulls a sheet closer to see) who the Hell is that? I don't even know a Steven Fletcher! Are you sure...?

Auditor: Calm down, Mr. Steele. Your employment returns were flagged by the computer because many of the employee names do not match with the listed Social Security Numbers. In the case of this Mr. Fletcher, the SSN provided to us returned this name. So, either the name is wrong or the number is wrong. Both cannot be right. In the case of the others, the numbers don't match anything and are probably just made up.

Buck: You are insinuating that my employees have

perpetrated a fraud? Listen, lady, these guys might not be the sharpest knives in the drawer, but smearing their reputations in front of their boss is a pretty low blow. What are we supposed to do? Give them the third degree in the middle of a hurricane so that we are 1000% sure their federal number is correct? This smacks of another time, like the '30's and another place... like Germany!

Auditor: Mr. Steele! I'm not sure how you meant that last...

Buck: Ok, Ok, I'll accept your tepid apology this time, but watch yourself. This is an official inquiry and I expect you to behave accordingly.

Auditor: But, but, WE are the ones making the inquiry!

Buck: Precisely! Now about this scurrilous accusation you are making about my management team....

Auditor: We aren't making, or, I am not making any...

Buck: Don't start back-pedaling now, you're on a roll. While you slander my whole staff, why don't you just give me the name and number of the regional supervisor for the U.S. Department of Labor? I'll draft the complaint while we finish up here. We should have a date set for district court by the time you go to lunch.

Auditor: Mr. Steele, will you sign this affidavit stating that your information is, to the best of your knowledge accurate as presented? If you can do that, I will conclude the audit.

Buck: Oh, OK.

Well, it was Wednesday afternoon and the paychecks had been presented, signed, returned and cash dispensed. This was always a tough one to call. If you paid the guys at night, chances are the money would be liquefied and gone by morning, quickly transferred to some bar cash register. If you pay 'em in the morning, they might disappear before the work gets done. That's the way society is and that's why bars are open late, for the convenience of the patrons, and stability of businesses everywhere. Banks, on the other hand, are not open for the convenience of patrons. That is why bars are, in general, better gauges and measures of a healthy society than banks.

Buck's cash receipts were hitting the high water mark and it was time to get them changed into a cashier's check or face a clumsy robbery attempt. He would have to bug into town for a few minutes and turn in this dough. As he approached the Woodstock Bank, Buck noticed two burly guys standing, no, loitering on the street corner. They looked like dicks, Buck thought, by both definitions; Bank dick and just plain unpleasant person, dick. He dismounted his Ford truck and made for the bank door. Both burly types were coming up from behind. Buck went straight to the nearest teller window and shoved his grimy moneybag against the glass.

"Excuse me, miss, I would like a cashier's check for $14,000. Here is my adding machine tape and coin tally slip. Oh, do you know these two guys drooling on my back?" Buck gestured to the two, just now pressing against him in line.

"Yes, of course. This is our bank manager, Mr. Messer and our security manager, Mr. Schlink." The teller introduced them like this was a social event.

The bank manager piped up first. "Sir, we are just interested to know why you have so much cash in your possession and in this form?"

Buck was still processing the fact that this dopey looking guy three minutes ago looked like a mugger on the corner but is actually the bank manager. "What do you mean? Why do I have money, a lot of money, or cash money? I own a carnival and we take in cash receipts. For safety, we turn these cash receipts into check form. Are you taking a survey or something? Have I won anything?" Buck was a little tired and getting prickly. "Are cashier's checks available here or should I look in the yellow pages?"

The bank manager was not backing off. "Your name is...?"
"Steele."
"Well, Mr. Steele we are not accustomed to seeing a large quantity of money arrive in a bag in this condition..."

"What? The bag or the money? I can't account for the condition of either. You see, I run a carnival. We work outdoors or in tents. Mostly outdoors. That's why they call it the outdoor amusement business, by the way. So, unlike this snug little bank you have here, we collect money in small transactions, day and night and in all weather conditions. The stuff gets wet, dirty, smelly and torn. Just like the hands that give it to us. It's still "legal tender for all debts, public and private", as it says on the green ones here." Buck pointed one of his dirty hands at crumpled dollars.

"Well, Mr. Steele, we can never be too careful. After all, we didn't actually see you come from the carnival. In fact, we didn't even know there was a carnival in the area."

"You probably didn't actually see the gas station owner leave his gas station or the grocery store guy actually leave the banana isle either, did you? You have some kind of phobia about money? I'll roll the coins for you, but you can forget about pressing the paper stuff. I just don't have the time..." The bank manager could also forget about any free ride tickets.

"Alright, Mr. Steele. Pardon the intrusion, we just have to watch out for anything unusual."

"With your attitude, the only unusual thing might be seeing customers at all. So how much for the cashier's check? Three dirty, wet dollars?"

Man, this town sure has an attitude. Earlier in the week, Buck had wanted to rent a vacant lot to park the carnival trucks on. This is an everyday procedure and most vacant lot owners jump at the chance to generate cash flow. The lot in question was big enough to accommodate all the trucks safely away from the road and any pedestrian areas. Buck contacted the property manager:

"How 'ya doin'? My name is Buck Steele." Buck thrust his hand out to shake with the property manager's. "I'm with Steele's Amusements and we are interested in paying you rent on your lot to park our trucks." His hand was still suspended in mid air, no handshake in the works yet.

"I'm well aware of who you are, or what you are Mr. Steele." The property manager was terse and kept his arms to his sides. We are not interested in renting our lot to you. In fact, we aren't interested in even seeing your filthy trucks and equipment around here."

Buck brought his outstretched hand back from the friendly position. "Is that straight from Mr. Gould or are you being weird all on your own here?" Buck was aware that the land was owned by Chester Gould, the cartoonist responsible for the comic strip, *Dick Tracy*.

"I speak for Mr. Gould in all matters of real-estate management. I'm afraid we have nothing more to discuss." The manager spun and stalked off.

Woodstock, Illinois was and is horse country. The rich folks there take great pride in the ownership of thoroughbreds and standards and the bragging rights that go with them. Buck always wondered why the owners of animals that produced so much smelly crap felt that theirs didn't. Steele's would find another parking space for its trucks. Buck could think of a few places that Mr. Gould could put *Dick Tracy* too.

Woodstock now held two strikes against them. First they suspected Steele's money to be dirty, then stated point blank that their trucks were. Buck would cop to the charge of dirty money. That was a literal truth, but not a legal one. But to call their trucks filthy was a low blow. Have they seen their fair grounds? Did this stinking town even have a decent truck wash? Moving on to the next stop would be a pleasure.

Moving money around to where it was needed was always a chore. Since the carnival was always on the move, normal banking privileges were non-existent. Buck had to resort to unconventional means to pay for things and people. One problem was advancing money to ride guys to get them to the carnival location. Some of these guys were either on the run from the law, hiding from an ex-wife or traveling with a very bad habit. Enter Western Union. Something similar to the much despised payday loan business started here. For a mere ten to twenty percent of the amount transferred, Buck could wire money to a wayward employee to bring them in. Buck never liked forking over the usurious amount to Western Union, but it was the only way to send money to a guy that had no bank account and only dealt in cash.

"So where are you?" Buck asked Corky over a bad phone connection.

"For purposes of sending money, I'm at..." Corky recited a bogus address. Probably somebody's mailbox or front porch that he had access to.

"How much is a ticket to Rockford?" Buck wanted to finish this quickly.

"Plane?"

"That'll be the day. No, on the running dog bus. How much to get you here?"

Buck knew better than to overshoot this expense estimate. Give Corky even a few bucks extra and he'll never show up.

"I think the ticket is about twelve bucks. Maybe you could send me a little extra so I could..." Corky was clipped short by Buck's impatience.

"OK, here's what I'll do. I'm gonna wire twenty bucks by

Western Union and they'll skim off five bucks to send it. That leaves you fifteen to get here. I better see you by day after tomorrow or you are in deep shit."; The usual Steele's warning.

"So I will owe you fifteen bucks?" Corky was getting cute.

"No, you'll owe me the whole twenty. The wire charge is yours, and quit trying to be funny." Buck cradled the phone and headed for the W.U. office. This was beginning to be a common occurrence.

Someday there will be a better way, but for now Steele's would have to trust carnival workers a few dollars at a time. The hope was that the carny worker would not blow all of his money at once and then continue to borrow. That hope was seldom turned to reality. In fact, on occasion there was an irresistible urge for L.E. Steele or Gramps, as he was known to try and reverse the cash flow process.

L.E. was a famous skinflint. Since this is the '70's the word entrepreneur applies. While his grandson Buck ran the carnival with Uncle Ray and Vinnie, L.E. would develop schemes to recover cash from the employees.

"Notice that the blade metal goes clean through the handle. That's quality boys." Gramps was demonstrating a Bowie knife to a group of ride guys gathered for the purpose of being fleeced by the master. "And," Gramps continued in smooth transition, "the sheath is designed for quick draw. Nosir, nobody is ever gonna get the drop on you if you carry this knife!" The sale was closed. All of the boys forked over their last ten bucks to get a genuine Bowie knife.

Later, Buck noticed that all of the boys were walking around with huge knives strapped to their legs. The things looked like machetes. What lunatic told them they could be seen carrying weapons on the fairgrounds? Oh, no. Gramps. Buck was steaming. Most of the ride guys were hotheaded enough without throwing gasoline on top of the situation. This was dangerous. Where the Hell was Gramps?

Buck found his granddad under a tent counting his money. "Buckie, I buy 'em for five and sell 'em for ten. What's wrong with that? It's just good business."

Jesus, the old man was getting daft. "You mean you buy deadly weapons for five and sell them for ten dollars of OUR money. Do you remember that all of these guys owe us until the end of the season? How long will they last with these things strapped to their legs without killing each other or going to jail? It would be good business if it wasn't here or with these guys. You oughta know better..." Buck really didn't like dressing down Gramps like this, but the old guy had done something loony.

"Well I'm not gonna refund anybody. This was a straightforward business deal and you can't tell me what to do. In fact, some of the boys haven't paid yet, so I have to keep all the money to insure my take. The old man had dug in his heels. Still, Buck would have to disarm the troops or face big trouble later on.

"OK, this is over for now. Don't sell anything more to the guys. None of them can afford it. Trust me." Buck went to gather up the guys and the knives. Good thing they weren't sold guns.

"I'll give 'em back at the end of the season. We can't have the fair people seeing us walking around looking like Davy Crockett. They'll be right here in the safe." Buck nodded toward the HQ trailer's safe. The boys were all standing around looking glum. Something about a foot-long blade hanging down their leg that appealed to them. Buck was spoiling the experience. "So put your names on the things and hand 'em over. No squawking."

Gramps was a carny of the old school. Money that was spent, either within the carnival or outside was never meant to stay gone. Whether through a card game, shell game, or some other mechanism, L.E. felt the imperative to retrieve his lost friends. All of them with pictures of presidents on them. To sell items to the employees was just a way of bringing the money back home. He didn't trust banks because they didn't like you to visit your money. You couldn't see it or feel it. The Depression didn't help matters either, so L.E. and then Al, Sr. and even Buck never put full faith in banks. Neither a borrower nor lender be. Live and die with cash.

Winter Quarters

Valparaiso, Indiana, 1970

This 'Vale of Paradise' was the home base of Steele's Amusements. Carnivals have to spend their off-season recovering from tour by repairing the rides, trucks and preparing for the next year. Many carnivals spend the off-season down South, either in Florida or, like Ernie Farrow's crew, between Mississippi and the East coast.

Valpo may be colder than Hell in the winter, but it was home and the Steele's were too busy in the winter to worry about the cold anyway. All the trucks needed to be gathered up from wherever they broke down and brought back to the big barn at Winter Quarters. Some always seemed to give up the ghost around

Rockford, Illinois at the end of the season; like the crew, exhausted. Buck would have to go and retrieve these before the cops did, then get them back to Indiana.

Each year the crew started to wander into Winter Quarters during March. The main building was a massive masonry barn with a domed roof and huge loft. The boys would show up earlier than necessary in the spring because there were steady meals and a place to flop. Even though the loft was unheated and March was still nasty in Northwest Indiana, this was a family homecoming of sorts. The loft was the bunkhouse. Thirty ride guys, and tradesmen would climb up the counter-weighted wood stairway to bunk on the plywood floor under the rafters. This was not exactly designed for human occupancy. There was no fire escape, no heat, and a lone toilet fixture on the ground level. It was a basic crash pad, for some very basic guys.

Uncle Ray had a few simple rules for the loft living Steele's crew. True to his Marine background, these rules were not open to varieties of interpretation. They were presented more than once to the boys in the loft to avoid confusion, and rule number one was: You will never take a lit cigarette or lit anything up into the loft. There were all of the flammables a carnival needs stored right where the boys slept. There was no fire escape leading from the loft. There was only one way down, and it was the unprotected wooden stairway. The Marine had spoken, and all those that knew him understood. Except one.

Hank and the boys had placed a booze order with one of their girlfriends who just happened to be going right by Semento's Tavern. This was convenient, since Steele's employees weren't allowed cars at Winter Quarters. The 'no car rule' was essential. Steele's had to know where the boys were and be ready to put the carnival on the road without an unnecessary head count. If the boys had wheels, it would be like herding cats to get them where they needed to be.

That night everybody was having a good time including Hank. They played poker and drank until they couldn't see or comprehend the cards. Hank lit a cigarette and staggered up the wooden steps to the loft. His body crumbled into his bedroll as cigarette ashes flew above him. Hank stared up at the rafters for a few minutes, noticing that there were now twice as many as before. He clumsily ground out his nearly done Lucky Strike into the plywood loft floor. He passed out.

The next day, one of the sober ride guys from the previous

night clued Uncle Ray in on the cigarette infraction. Ray took the snitch at his word and the news calmly, or so it would seem. Ray always seemed to take adverse information in a calm manner. It didn't make sense to react without thinking the situation through. Ray had learned to survive the war in the South Pacific by doing just that. Think your way through a problem and keep your head.

Night came and the boys crashed in the loft at intervals. Hank likewise. At four o'clock in the morning, Uncle Ray crept along the outer wall of the Winter Quarters barn. He was totally silent. It was totally dark. Ray ascended the wooden steps to the loft as quietly as he had crept through the jungles of Okinawa many years before. He slid into the bedroll next to the comatose Hank. It seemed like a dream Hank was having: He was in a fight with some kids and they were throwing rocks, big rocks and hitting him in the chest. The pain was unbearable. Hank was in agony. The pain roused him from his sleep to discover that kids weren't throwing rocks at him, but Ray was pummeling him with his fists. First there was the shock of waking nose-to-nose with your boss in bed. Then there was the excruciating pain as your boss beat the tar out of you. Hank had the wind knocked out of him from a blow to the sternum. He wanted to gasp, but couldn't because his lungs had been purged of air. The punches kept coming as Hank curled into a ball and prayed his lungs would fill. This only gave Ray a new slate of targets to pound with his fists. There was no human language being used at this point. Ray was silent death. Hank was yelping out animal sounds as the other ride boys woke up. The fusillade of blows stopped only when Ray's arm was tired.

When morning came, Maytha Steele had laid out the long tables in Winter Quarters with a substantial breakfast. The entire crew was fed family style twice each day in the barn. Up in the loft Hank felt his ribs. He was sure some were cracked. Jesus, what had he done to deserve such a beating? Oh, yeah, he had broken rule number one. The meaning of Lucky Strike changed for Hank from then on. He understood that risking a fire and the lives of the crew wouldn't be allowed. A common law had been enforced, and punishment meted out.

Hank staggered down the loft steps slowly; one at a time. At the bottom of the steps he ran right up against Uncle Ray, the Marine. Ray smirked, "How 'ya doin'?

"Uh, OK, I think." Hank was nearly speechless.

"Good. Oh, remember about the cigarettes...." Ray said matter-of-factly as he walked away and over to the table. Ray had made an impression that was hard to forget. The soldiers in the unit were back in line.

The itinerary had been laid out during the winter and the spots booked. Between the fair board meetings, and the carnival industry's Outdoor Amusement Business Association meeting in Gibsonton, Florida, Steele's Amusements had finally lined up a complete season's tour. There were a huge number of things to be done before putting all the equipment on the road. The trucks had to be painted. Crippins was going to be on that whenever he sobered and showed up. The rides had scores of welds to be fixed. Either from vibration or overloading of large customers, the metal on certain rides had fatigued and cracked. The trailers had to be prepped. The reverse process of winterization was for some reason more work than winterizing in the first place. The lines had to be blown out and holding tanks emptied. The bunk trailer that served as home for the ride boys had to be prepared. Everything had to be done to allow the entire crew to live in the wilds of Wisconsin and Illinois for months.

Vinnie Steele, Ray's brother had brought in a load of clear pine to carve some decorations for the band organ. The loud, obnoxious organ was a beautiful thing to behold but a pain to hear for more that a few minutes. A carnival has to have ambience and that damn organ was pure ambience. When Vinnie and the boys put the instrument into its special new trailer it seemed to lose its antique appeal, so the craftsman Steele went about hand carving decoration, finials, and appliqués to beautify the exterior.

Meanwhile, Buck spent his leisure time on the hunt for slum. No, not the low cost housing kind, but the cheap carnival prizes that players get for losing or winning small. This was not an easy task, finding little plaster figurines, dolls, wooden toys that looked like they were worth having but cost next to nothing. Finding this material was an art. Finding it in carnival quantities was a survival skill. The economics of it demand that you buy the ubiquitous cupie doll or wooden cane for a dime or so, in volumes of thousands. A prize every time game did not mean it was a particularly valuable prize. All you had to do is keep a kid moderately happy. Buck was on the hunt. He knew of a Woolworth's store in a small town nearby that might be a possibility. Slum had to be something that was so hard for the store to sell that it was almost free. A few cents apiece for little statues, salt and pepper shakers, anything. Woolworth's had 'em in the back storeroom. Tossed in with boxes full of excelsior packing, dozens, hundreds of trinkets were flung all over the storage room.

Boxes were loaded with merchandise long since given up on. They would have thrown the stuff out if they had thought about it. This was a good slum find.

Buck could also count on Irving. Irving, a.k.a. Tiny was a guy that drove around with his car trunk full of toys and junk; a road peddler. He would meet Buck in a parking lot somewhere and sell him little Teddy Bears and things from his car for cash. Irving would do just about anything for cash. In WWII he was a pilot for the Flying Tigers in Southeast Asia. These mercenary types would blow up bridges and shoot down planes for a cash commission. Five hundred bucks for a bridge or up to a thousand depending on the plane shot down. So now Tiny, who really weighed about 300 pounds sold stuff out of his car.

The slum hunt would need to take a detour for now. Buck needed some hunting supplies and knew where to go. He would stop by Fetla's Outpost store and see what they could part with. Fetla's was one thing Valparaiso, Indiana was famous for. Worldwide, people that knew nothing of Indiana or the Midwest would know about the labyrinthine bazaar known as Fetla's Outpost. This was not a shop for the timid or paranoid. It was not a place to go if you were claustrophobic. Fetla's was a large store constructed like a maze, with merchandise piled to the ceiling. It was like walking into the souk in Casablanca. There was a scheme, some kind of organization but it was unknown to those that worked or shopped there. That was its charm and adventure.

Buck walked into Fetla's a weary man. He had a few extra minutes and needed to look for junk. Sure, 'slum' was one thing he needed, but Fetla's was a place that you went to search for survivors. It was akin to an earthquake site, where merchandise was piled, tossed, thrown, and crammed into every available place. This was actually an ingenious marketing strategy. Shoppers would go, not to examine articles in some orderly fashion, but to excavate. The desire to dig is very strong in Homo sapiens, and at Fetla's, you could tap into that ancient DNA and discover. Discover. Buck started to rout through some pile of military surplus clothing when he noticed what looked like a rocket launcher standing on end by the edge of a table. Fetla's was the kind of place where lethal military gear did not seem out of place. Actually, there were more racks loaded with rifles, bazookas, machine guns, and grenade launchers than in any store in the country. It was a fact that this was the largest arms dealer in the Midwest. Most local residents assumed that these items of weaponry were all for sale legally. Perhaps, in the unregulated

1970's environment they were, but part of the excitement of Fetla's was that you thought this was a frontier outpost, perched on the thin edge of the law. There was the possibility that these weapons were just a little too powerful to be sold in this way. This place was fun. It was easy to get sidetracked in one area and then actually buy something you had never thought of before. Such was the lure of the deal. Next to the clothing items you might find rat poison or a rack of porno magazines, or cat food. Turn around and pick up a high-powered deer rifle and a canoe paddle. Life preservers were next to the Thermos bottles, which were next to the baby formula. There was an organization to it, but only from a warped, dyslexic perspective. And then there was the 'good stuff'. It was well known to the locals that the good stuff was in another building. This was very hush-hush and known only to the *insiders*. You had to know somebody special to even ask the question about the good stuff and where it might be found. The good stuff, it was rumored, referred to military gear of a higher order. Also, again rumored, some explosives not generally available anywhere. But if you knew the boys at Fetla's, and if you could keep your mouth shut, you might be let in on some of this select merchandise. Was it legal? Probably, but they weren't proud of that fact. If this stuff were not special, if its possession was not problematic, would they keep it in another building? The élan and, in fact, the interest was generated by the suspicion that you were about to buy contraband. Maybe it was only contraband if purchased in England or some pacifist country, but as long as it was illicit somewhere, people wanted it.

So as Buck was fondling what seemed to be a grenade launcher a youngish sales clerk approached him. This was unusual, because the sales people generally stayed behind the largest handgun display in the state. They stayed in back of a massive glass display case showing, caressing and discussing the finer points of GUNS.

"Anything I can help you find, sir? The clerk was patronizing.

"If you can find anything here you are a better man than me." Buck quipped. "But I was looking for hunting accessories when I came in. Just for curiosity, you know those penny toys, the little plastic things that you have by the box?"

"If we have 'em, they're over by the snow blowers. Some guy was in here a little while ago and bought a few cases though. We might be out."

"Story of my life. You got any frog spears?"

"Yeah, they were over by the plastic toys, in a barrel." The clerk was sort of dead panned. Reminded Buck of Sgt. Friday. Just the facts.

Having depleted the possibilities here, Buck needed to search for some hardware at the shop of last resort. Wark's Hardware in Valpo was in a time warp. Old man Wark, he was always an old man, had stuff that couldn't be found anywhere else. The reason for this is that he never sold anything. His front display window still held dry goods and hardware from the '20s. If you were looking for parts for something that hadn't been made in 40 years or so, you could still find 'em at Wark's.

"Mister Wark!" Buck banged the spring-loaded door on the way into the store. "Do you have any welding materials? I have this really old..." As Buck was about to explain the thing he needed he heard the standard line from Wark.

"Oooh, that would be nice, but I don't think we do. If we did, it would be over here." The ancient Wark glided into the back of the store with an arm pointing ahead of him. This was the usual route right to the thing you were looking for. Wark never got rid of anything.

Procurement ended. It was time to do a final checklist and put this show on the road Steele's Amusements, that is.

Community Relations Rockford, Illinois

The 'patch' is the guy that fixes public relations problems in a carnival. This usually falls on the owner of the business or the lot manager. The lot manager in a carnival is always circulating the midway looking for problems. The goal is to diffuse a situation before it becomes a matter of bail money, or a felony.

As towns go, Rockford, Illinois is a pretty nice one. It has its ritzy areas, and not so ritzy ones. The mayor loves the city and does his best to keep a lid on things. But one day things came a little unglued. This was back when Buck's dad Al, Sr. was alive and Steele's Amusements was playing the Kishwaukee Avenue Association carnival. This was an important gig. It ran two weeks and was a big money maker. Steele's had run into a snag once before. Some years back they wanted to put the usual advertising in the local newspaper announcing the carnival dates and information. The paper, believing that Rockford would suffer from this degenerate form of entertainment, refused to accept the advertising.

"And you have justification to refuse this ad on what legal basis?" Al, Sr. was probing the advertising editor's mind. It seemed that the paper's position was becoming less amenable to discussion.

"Mr. Steele, we can refuse advertising copy based on any standard we like. We are rejecting this ad."

"OK, so let me get this straight. You are objecting to this particular content or ad copy? Or are you objecting to a carnival wanting to advertise in your paper?" Al's head was beginning to ache. "If you are saying you don't like the copy, why don't we just edit it? This is a newspaper. You do edit things don't you? In fact, don't they call your job 'advertising editor?' This all seems pretty simple to me." Yup, Al was going to need brain surgery if this didn't straighten out fast. The pain in his head was either caused by editorial stupidity or an evil demon within his skull. It was impossible to tell which, at this point.

"Yes, Mr. Steele, this paper objects to the ad copy and the purpose of the ad. As a rule, we don't like to advertise for carnivals. They bring a certain element into the community and we don't want to promote that." The advertising editor had his nose in the air and was looking down on Al at the same time; some trick.

"OK, you're making this pretty clear for me, so I will make this clear for you. Get together with your boss, the publisher of this rag and discuss which is more objectionable: A carnival playing in your town, or both of you sitting in court for the better part of a year. While you're at it, pick up a copy of the Constitution of the United States and check out the first amendment that you come to. It's a short read and won't take up much of your valuable time. And one more thing: This carnival is coming to your prissy, pristine little town. If you don't want to be sued for the damages your advertising refusal may cause, just take your time and blow us off. We either get our money from ticket sales or a court judgement. I don't care which." Al walked. This was not going to be an easy week.

Oddly enough, the publisher contacted Al Sr. a few days later with some face saving line about a mix-up and the ad copy was fine. They would run the ad and gladly take Steele's Amusements money. Problem solved, but in the minds of Al Steele and his son, Buck an axiom was formed: Rockford is a tight-assed, political town. Watch 'em carefully.

Fast-forward a decade or two to when Buck was running the show. It was his turn to negotiate the rough waters of the Rockford upper-middle class. They were booked to run the carnival for a week in the parking lot of a very nice shopping center. This was near the best part of town. The elite neighborhood of Rockford. Steele's was invited to set up by a local not-for-profit group. The fund-raiser was going to help the group achieve their financial goals and Steele's to meet their financial obligations. Even the Rotary Club likes this kind of arrangement.

The Steele's Amusement trucks rolled into Rockford, Illinois. It's quite a parade if you're there to see it. Uncle Ray had already scoped out the parking lot. The layout was plotted with precision. Just the sight of twenty-odd trucks painted orange and cream screaming into town at high speed is pretty exciting. This did not go unnoticed by the Rockford upper crust. They were primed for a dispute and Buck, the patch knew it.

The first night of operations went smoothly. There was a

big turnout and the accompanying noise of screaming kids could be heard for quite a distance. The band organ was pumping out that weird military music and the ride machinery was producing its own melody. Carnival lights kept the neighborhood aglow until midnight. Next day, all Hell broke loose.

The mayor of Rockford, a man who loved his city, came rushing to the Steele's office trailer early and in person. He was purple-faced mad and was spitting as he yelled at Buck about the level of noise this 'damn carnival' was making. His constituents, the town's most elite residents were up in arms over the noise, dirt, and rowdiness brought by Steele's Amusements. The mayor demanded that the carnival shut down and leave town immediately.

Of course, this would be a problem, Buck thought. It sounds simple to just blow town and forget that anything happened. But then, where would they go? They planned on being in Rockford for the week and Steele's had a huge crowd of employees and expenses tied up in the job. Buck calmly explained the various factors in play.

"Mr. Mayor, can I call you Harvey? How 'bout Harv? You see all these guys working around here? If I go and tell them: Contrary to what you were thinking at the beginning of the week, you are not working this week and won't be paid... These guys will hit the proverbial roof. They all have families to feed and bad habits to support. This carnival is their livelihood. Actually, it's my livelihood too, but the difference is I have a bank account that can stretch until next week. These people," Buck waved his arm across the panorama of Steele's employees, "haven't been as fortunate as me. They are living from day-to-day and stopping them now would be a personal tragedy for each and every one of them." Buck was running at full steam now. The Mayor was stuck in heavy rhetorical mud. "Another factor is that a fine community group in Rockford has placed their trust in Steele's Amusements to stabilize their financial situation. Mr. Mayor, this is a fund-raiser. We were invited to your city to help raise awareness, raise money and provide some fun for the kids at the same time. Now, what can we do to improve the situation, as you see it?"

"We need to shut down this carnival..." The Mayor kept to the line. What was he? Narcoleptic? Did he sleep through what Buck had just told him?

"Mayor, I know *that* is what the old biddies on the hill have laid on you, but we have to come up with a reasonable solution here. We don't have the luxury of washing this business out of town and waiting to see what damage forty pissed off men can do in five days. Listen, this shopping center is situated right on a major U.S. highway. If being on Hwy 20 doesn't bother anybody, with all of its noise and exhaust fumes, I can't see that a week of carnival activity should change things much. Where is the offended party?" Buck put a hand up to blot out the sun and made like he was looking for the Rockford Social Committee up on the hill.

The Mayor, Harv, had a suggestion: "Mr. Steele, you're looking in the right direction. The neighborhood up there..." Harv pointed vaguely. "That is where the complaints have originated. They are claiming public nuisance, disturbing the peace and so forth. Let's go and talk to them and see what we can do." Finally, some daylight breaks in the governmental mind.

The Mayor climbed into his Continental and with Buck headed up the hill, the Mayor jerking the huge car back and forth barely keeping control. As they hit the summit, the Mayor recognized a woman in her driveway unloading luxury goods from her luxury car. Pay-dirt, Buck thought. Pulling up in the drive, Harv hit the 'all windows down' control, making it clear he did not expect to get out of the vehicle. Buck, on the other hand, jumped out of the still rolling Continental and approached the woman.

Harv tossed the beast in Park and spoke up first. "Mary, this is Mr. Steele, the owner of the carnival we were talking about. He wanted to address your complaints and offer some possible solutions."

Buck knew it was charm-time and kicked on the neon smile. If his blue eyes, thirty-two year old body and blonde hair don't work this time, they're all screwed. "Nice to meet you." The carny's hand extended to press the flesh.

Mary, or whatever her name was looked suspicious. "I don't believe that you are associated with that carnival, Mr. Steele is it?" Buck wasn't letting go of her hand. Prolonged personal contact. A risky social move, but this situation called for bold action.

"Of course I am, ma'am. In fact, I represent the third generation of Steele's in this business." Buck left out discussion of the forth generation so as not to confuse the woman. "I realize that the charity fund-raiser is causing some inconvenience to you and your neighbors. We think we can tamp the noise down just a bit if you give us a chance. Why don't you bring the kids down (this was a tactical move, she obviously could bring grandkids or even great grandkids...) to the midway for some free fun. I can set you up with a stack of ticket books and the kids can ride all afternoon..." Buck was cut off abruptly.

Mary, thinking she was Queen Mary said, "You'll need to do better than 'tamp the noise down a bit' to get our votes Mayor. We told you that this is a police matter and that you had better handle it. The Mayor went slack-jawed. Mary's rabies vaccination was over due.

"Look, Steele, we will need you to shut down..."

"OK, here's is what we can do if you will play along here." Buck the patch was pulling out a settlement scheme: "We will close down all the game concession joints and maybe a few rides to reduce the noise level. That will also reduce the amount of light, since the booths will be taken down. It amounts to half of the revenue from this job, but at least we could absorb the employees into other work right here and keep 'em out of trouble. You do want to keep them out of trouble, don't you Harv?"

The Mayor was seeing that this might work in his favor. A political decision. "Sure, Buck, I think we can give that a shot. Hey, about those ticket books..." More grease for the Rockford machine.

The rest of the show should go OK, since some previous planning was in place. The local newspaper was pacified. One of the carnival employee's mother was now married to the editor. If the paper kicked up too much a fuss, they would just trot out the Mortician, as the employee was known and get them to cool it.

Model Citizens

"I think they are here, Mr. Lucky." Uncle Vinnie was smart-assing some news to Buck that was not welcome. The Model Carnival Owners Association was stopping by for their yearly field trip. These weasels would drop in for three days of photos, hobnobbing with carnies and general sponging. This was an invasion and Buck was the host.

    The modelers dropped in to the Columbia County Fair in Portage Wisconsin and wanted the royal treatment. Maybe the idea was that they would promote the carnival by replicating the rides in small scale? Or were they just geeks with an obsession about making things small? Whatever the reason, the Director of the Outdoor Amusement Business Assn. suggested that Steele's treat these enthusiasts gently. As OABA Director Kunz put it: "Outside of the carnival business, these guys are the only thing we have going for us...." There is something to be said for being a fan club to a beleaguered business. The Consumer Product Safety Commission, various state boards and one particularly testy Massachusetts congressman always seemed to be getting up the collective carnival nose. So maybe some guys building carnivals out of tiny pieces of plastic and wood were harmless enough. Some good PR might be in order. Buck decided to feed 'em.

The modelers expected to be wined and dined at the Cookhouse, and so they were. Plied with corn dogs, popcorn, and a weird soda concoction, the modelers were wallowing in their element. They also were given prime space and exclusive access to the carnival midway, after hours. They were treated like family...as all welcome guests were, and provided camping sites to park their rigs, pound in some stakes and pitch their tents.

Buck watched the modelers as they gleefully measured their favorite rides and plotted to violate all forms of intellectual property rights owned by the ride manufacturers. They meticulously gauged each component of a ride, transcribed data to worksheets and drew up blueprints. Could this have been a very clever reverse-engineering ploy by Chinese spies? Were the secrets of the Tilt-A-Whirl and Rock-O-Plane being smuggled out of the country? Should the FBI be called?

Buck figured most of these guys were refugees of the model train cult. He saw some subtle signs in them of *HO Scale Syndrome*: pants too short, t-shirts too tight, baseball caps with little trains on them, etc...

As the day wore on, the chief modeler, Hans sidled up to one of Steele's custom ride trailers, used to transport specific rides, like the Scrambler. Now he was getting dangerously close to some prime trade secrets. Buck had devised a system to dismantle, transport, and then reassemble certain rides for best time savings and efficiency. A carnival is all about hitting the ground running. Transport and assembly of rides is an engineering art and science, and Buck was the best welder-lawyer anywhere. So what was this guy up to?

The model boys cycled back to the Cookhouse. It seems that blueprinting is serious work and they needed to refuel. Foot-long hotdogs and the proprietary soda drink were on the menu and they all dove in.

The next day, final plans were being transcribed and the modelers eyed their next stop. Portage, Wisconsin had yielded a load of data, and they had it all on paper. One last sortie to the

Cookhouse provided the "...hit the road breakfast." Much like guests in China being offered green tea, from that day forward, the phrase became synonymous with guests being gently ushered off the property.

Gibtown, Florida, U.S.A.

Much is made of Gibsonton, Florida and the way the town accepts its carnival residents. The zoning ordinances are well known to favor the sideshow carnies by allowing them to park their equipment, sets and themselves just about anywhere they own.

The place looks decidedly low rent, but that is why overwintering show people go there; to live economically until the traveling season begins again. It is a matter of pride that a homeowner may have tons of carnival rides rusting in the front yard. The level of detritus is considered a testament to one's dues paid in the business. Carnival baggage is something they all carry and the stories they convey are equally as heavy.

One such story is that of Grady Stiles, the Lobster Boy.

When you are born with claws rather than hands, you might be excused for a bad attitude. But if you add serious alcohol to the mix, Grady became a grade-A low-life. He killed and he was killed.

Ectrodactyly; The genetic condition of having lobster claws for hands and feet. This doesn't mean that the *pinchers* were weak or non-functional in any way. Grady's claws were like the jaws of a vice, as the story goes. And when he wanted to abuse someone, he could clamp on and inflict extreme pain.

Fred Rosen in his book, *Lobster Boy: The Bizarre Life and Brutal Death of Grady Stiles Jr.*, described at great length the life and times of Gibtown's most infamous resident. The sordid details of, first the murder committed by Stiles and then his own subsequent murder played out over several year's time in central Florida.

Stiles presented the darker side of Gibtown, but in order to see its best side, you have to look at it through a different lens.

The carnies are dedicated to a cheerful profession by design. The goal is to Amaze!, Astonish! and Thrill! In the winter, the carnival owners and vendors drop into Gibtown to rejoin their friends and associates. It is a time to socialize and also nail down *spots* or contracts for the next traveling carnival season.

Many show owners have left something of themselves behind to display at the American Carnival Museum. You need to go to the American Carnival Museum. Call ahead if you need a special appointment, but make that call. Thousands of photographs of the American Traveling Carnival are in the archive. Banners, rides and even model rides are displayed. The whole history of the traveling carnival is offered up to thrill and amaze. It's ALIVE!

The story of the carnival sideshow is represented by the life of Ward Hall, Gibtown denizen. The modern day P.T. Barnum of the carnival business, Ward will soon be immortalized in a biography by Tim O'Brien, *Ward Hall - King of the Sideshow*. If you wanted to know anything about the carnival sideshow, about an act, about where an act could be found or what alternatives to an act there were; Ward Hall was your man. He's done it all and seen it all.

Although the carnival sideshow has nearly disappeared from traveling shows, their past still lives in the work of Hall and others and shown about Gibtown.

For a glimpse of the history of traveling carnivals, see my essay, *The American Traveling Carnival*, by Kenneth L. Miller available on Amazon.com

In this small Florida town, the carnies always had a place to call their own. In the words of an unidentified carnival worker:

"The season came, the season went. All my money I have spent. No cookhouse, no job, No- vember!" (Gibtown Audio Books) In Steele's Amusements as in many other carnivals, the ride boys and other seasonal staff needed a place to hang out all winter. Gibtown.

Uncle Bob at the Hi-Striker…

Wilmot Wisconsin fair

Ray and Al Steele Sr.

Portage, Wisconsin Carnival

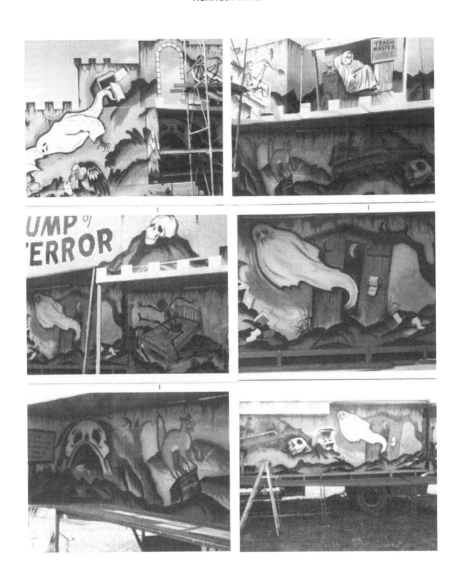

The Dark Ride

Winter Quarters, Valparaiso, Indiana 1959
A work in progress...

Columbus County Fair

The Thing, a ride

L.E. Steele's Starting Job with Bodart Shows

Tickets, by Harry C.

The coin of the realm...comp tickets

Buck Steele, shearing the "Frog"

The Band Organ Trailer, by Vinnie Steele

L.E. Steele selling Pony Ride Tickets

The Famous Steele's Band Organ

Uncle Vinnie's erection truck; engineering and design by self-taught Vinnie Steele.

The custom-made Scrambler trailer, a Steele invention

Left photo:
Buck Steele, third from the left and his wife, Judy in front. 1967

Right photo:
 Buck Steele, on the left as a newborn being held by an authentic American Indian, named Johnny Cake. 1936
 The photo was taken at L.E. Steele's "Mug Joint" at the Wisconsin Dells. L.E. started in business during the Great Depression taking portrait photos at resorts and fairs throughout the Midwest.

Somewhere in the American Carnival Museum is a small sample of Steele's Amusements ephemera. The photo shows some advertisement for the carnival and the most important piece of daily accounting record; The draw book tracked a handful of one-dollar bills disbursed to each ride boy every morning. It was a cash advance that paid for their food throughout the working portion of the day and money for smokes as well.

Epilogue

Steele's Amusements came to an end as a traveling carnival in the 1970's. Each of the Steeles moved into different endeavors; the ride boys went on to join other carnivals and so did the tradesmen. Buck continued to be Buck, quixotic at times, but always fully engaged in local politics and business.

Tommy Steele's business card identified him as the "Famous Peddler"; and so he was. Tommy never forgot the bally. To this day, he can roll off his "talk" for Baby Flo Johnson, or the foot-long hot dogs, or even long tracts from 19th century poets. He developed and honed his verbal skills…all from Steele's Amusements.

Randy Steele, as a young man was the aristocrat of Steele's Amusements. Sometimes seen sporting an ascot tie, he was only a smoking jacket away from full Edwardian caricature. His higher social standards held him apart from the ride boys, but propelled him into a career in radio and then to Westinghouse.

Larry Steele, graduating from the "Nickel Pitch" or the "Lucky Strike" game, continued on to graduate from Indiana University Law. As U.S. Attorney for the Northern District of Indiana, Larry was a zealous defender of the interests of average Americans. His courtroom arguments are legendary. Larry was known to be an exasperating Devil's Advocate, as tough on his clients as he was on adversaries. But through this method of testing facts and theories, he almost always arrived at the truth; the core of legal enterprise.

Larry's mom, Charlotte Steele lived well past the days of the grab joints and foot-long hot dogs. In her 89 years she had also worked for Valparaiso University Food Services. It was important to Charlotte that the carnival was humane. She cared about everything, including the ponies in the pony ride.

Maytha Steele, Buck's mom, like Charlotte put the lie to a saying, "…the good die young." She lived to the age of 94, and was certainly good.

The brothers, Al Steele Sr., Ray Steele, and Vinnie Steele all left their indelible imprints on succeeding generations of

Steeles. It is a Steele trait to survive by taking charge of what you can and inventing what you need to. If the Great Depression can be credited with anything good, it would be instilling self-reliance, and the Steeles had that in abundance. The old man, L.E. Steele did what he had to do to survive and those Depression era skills lasted and instructed all who followed in his footsteps.

Acknowledgments

To acknowledge the storytellers is important, and so I will give credit where credit is due:

Once you get Al (Buck) Steele going, he is hard to stop. His depth of knowledge about the carnival and the outdoor amusement business is encyclopedic. I could listen to the guy for hours, days….and have. He is as open as they come and contributed enormously to this work.

Buck's wife, Marilyn served as a catalyst by inventing and hosting the occasions where these stories were shared. No small task…thanks.

Larry Steele represented the ideal of "carny makes good" and first introduced me to the business side of amusements. He thought I was an idiot for lumping circuses and carnivals together;

and he was right. The similarities are only superficial, and he set me straight.

Tommy Steele eerily reproduced the sound and chatter of a 1970 carnival. To listen to him put you on the midway at the time and made you want to go back there.

Randy Steele backed up the stories with his own take on them and served as the link to memories of his dad, Vinnie. Vinnie, Ray and Al Sr. were the brothers that made the show work.

However, it was their wives that made the "...show beautiful." Maytha, Charlotte and Margaret Steele raised their kids on the carnival and I had the distinct pleasure of listening to their stories before they passed away. If only the rest of the world could maintain their positive attitudes.

The Steele kids, Kathy, Kelly and Mary told honest stories of "grandma Maytha" in a way almost impossible to put into words, because we couldn't stop laughing.

Thanks to Smitty, the Steele's Amusements electrician for some of the more hair-raising details of the carnival.

And thanks most of all to my wife, Jory for putting up with my various avocations and obsessions. At least this was the most fun of them all.

Author
Kenneth L. Miller

Traveling the world in search of a good story. "Reading and research are the best part of the process." Ken is a Michigan native living in New Buffalo; Author of *Steele's Amusements, Carnival Life on the Midway* and the Kindle single, *The American Traveling Carnival*, available on Amazon.com

For more information, see millerbooks.com and steelesamusements.com

Steeles Amusements

Made in the USA
Charleston, SC
30 September 2013